The Warmest Tide: How Climate Change is Changing History

Sean Munger

CONTENTS

CHAPTER 1: THE END OF HISTORY?

Is climate change the end of the world, or the end of history?

No, it isn't. But understanding why it isn't, and how global warming has affected and will affect world history, has a lot to do with what you think history is, and how you look at the world.

In 1989, as Communism was collapsing, pundit and columnist Francis Fukuyama famously declared "the end of history." Two years later he was corrected by no less prominent a pop culture figure as Captain James T. Kirk of *Star Trek*, who answered, "We haven't run out of history quite yet." There's no question that global warming represents a fundamental shift in the tides of human history. Just how big that shift will be, and what it might mean for us in the future, is something that few people have really confronted in a rational and systematic way. That's what I want to do in this book.

Climate change clearly does have enormous implications for all aspects of our society—business and the economy most directly, but also our political system, the global order of nations, and our religious and spiritual institutions. One may, and people often do, look at various aspects of this change in isolation. Insurance companies and financial planners are looking at how climate change and its related threats will affect the bottom line. Military experts are examining how climate change will affect patterns of conflict and global competition for resources. Pope Francis I, in his famous encyclical *Laudato si'* from 2015, interrogated climate change from a theological perspective. But are any of these sectors—financial, political, religious—talking to each other?

I posit that it takes a historian to try to put climate change in its broadest and most meaningful context. Historians are trained to see the big picture and ask the big questions about how everything fits together. I can tell you with absolute certainty that the historians of the future will be looking backwards to our era—the 2010s and 2020s—with intense interest, because what we do now and how we adapt to the wave of societal-level change that is coming will be the historical basis for understanding whatever form the world and human society take as a result of climate change. But we who live in this time, and are trying to make a living and raise our children and hold on to what we've got, don't have the luxury of waiting 20, 50 or 100 years to make sense of what's happening now. Thus, a historian living today, in 2019 or 2020, has a duty to apply his or her trained historical thinking to the conditions of today and tell it like it is. That is why this book exists.

This book is intended to be short, sweet and no-nonsense. I'm going to start with a few basic questions about climate change and how it's affecting the world, our businesses and our institutions. I'm going to tell you a bit about its history—that part is often missed—and perhaps what we can expect. I'll tell you about some things that are ending, and some others that may be be-

Pope Francis I, *Laudato si'* (On Care For Our Common Home), Holy See, 2015

James Hansen et al., "Ice Melt, Sea Level Rise and Superstorms: The Threat of Irreparable Harm," in *Climate Science, Awareness and Solutions*, March 2016

David Houle & Tim Rumage, *This Spaceship Earth* (David A. Houle & Associates, 2015)

Intergovernmental Panel on Climate Change, First Report (1990), online

Paavo Järvensivu, Tero Toivanen, Tere Vadén et al., "Global Sustainable Development Report 2019, Invited Background Document on Economic Transformation, to Chapter: Transformation: The Economy," August 14, 2018, online (search at site at bios.fi)

Naomi Oreskes & Erik M. Conway, *Merchants of Doubt: How a Handful of Scientists Obscured the Truth on Issues from Tobacco Smoke to Global Warming* (Bloomsbury Press, 2010)

Nathaniel Rich, *New York Times Magazine*, "Losing Earth: The Decade We Almost Stopped Climate Change" (August 1, 2018)

Daniel Yergin, *The Prize: The Epic Quest for Oil, Money, and Power* (New York: Simon & Schuster, 1990)

ACKNOWLEDGMENTS

This book was written over a several month period at the end of 2018 and the first half of 2019, but it comes from a long period of study, teaching, introspection and self-realization that has been going on much longer than that. Although this is not an academic book, it does have roots in academia, and I wish to thank Matthew Dennis, my adviser for my dissertation *Ten Years of Winter: The Cold Decade (1810-1820) and Environmental Consciousness in the Early 19th Century*, which was my intellectual gateway into the subject of climate change. I also thank Dr. Alexander Dracobly, who championed the idea of me teaching a class on climate change, which pushed me through the gateway and onto the road. James Rodger Fleming, author of *Historical Perspectives on Climate Change*, has also been an inspiration.

Thanks also: Bob Leonard, David Houle, Wilford and Shandy Welch, Dorice Horenstein, Adam Rose, Christian Kaylor, Shouka Rezvani, my 6th and 7th grade classes, Andy Dowling, and especially Cody Climer.

ginning. I'll end with a potential vision of the future, not as prognostication, but as a reasoned guess about where climate change may be taking our history. That's what this book is and is intended to be.

Here's what it's *not*. It is not a polemic, a political tract designed to advance an ideology (or denigrate another). It's also not a jeremiad, a screed of apocalyptic doom intended to shock you (or anyone) into some kind of action. I come at climate change not with the pleading of an environmentalist, but with the temperance of historian. I speak often about climate change, and a reaction I commonly hear is something to the effect of, "I've never heard anyone talk about climate change like that before." I am not going to tell you to put a recycling bin in your kitchen or buy a Prius. There are plenty of books out there on climate change that are polemics or jeremiads, but this isn't one of them.

This also is not a science book. If you take a moment to thumb through it, you may be surprised to see not a single graph, chart or temperature map. Climate change has too long been dominated by data: sea level predictions, temperature averages and that sort of thing. You can't avoid some scientific concepts when talking about climate change, but that is a relatively minor aspect. You can't tell the story, say, of the manned Apollo landings on the Moon without touching on some scientific concepts, but imagine how much of the substance of that history you'd miss if the main focus of the story was on the physics of trans-lunar trajectories. If you want the science, go look it up. No one's hiding it.

Before we delve into the substance, I want to say one more thing, and it's the elephant in the room when it comes to climate change. And that is *fear*. Many people shut down when the subject of climate change comes up, because it's too big, too scary, and too paralyzing to grapple with. And so much media coverage is geared toward shock headlines—the aforementioned jeremiads—that it's no surprise that this is a common reaction. A friend once told me, "Thinking about climate change literally makes me want to die." I understand that reaction, but I think we need to move past it.

On the frigid morning of March 4, 1933, the newly-inaugurated President Franklin D. Roosevelt said, "Let me assert my firm belief that the only thing we have to fear is fear itself—nameless, unreasoning, unjustified terror which paralyzes needed efforts to convert retreat into advance." He may as well have been talking about climate change. Fear is our worst enemy, but it is an enemy that can be defeated.

There is hope regarding climate change—not merely hope that its worst effects can be avoided, but hope that we can build a better world, and better lives for ourselves, even (and especially) in the face of such an awesome challenge. We, the human race, are not simply going to lay down and die in the face of climate change. There's no precedent in history for such a decision, and much precedent for exactly the opposite—the resilience and ingenuity of human societies to adapt themselves to new and even drastically different circumstances. But if you need that affirmation now, before we get into the meat of the project, go ahead right now and turn to Chapter 9. I'll wait.

So do we, who live in the era of climate change, find ourselves truly facing "the end of history?" If I thought so, it would be pretty pointless for me to write this book, Global warming is a turning point in history, no doubt about it. But if you'll allow me to quote *Star Trek* again, this time Mr. Spock: "History is replete with turning points. You must have faith that the universe will unfold as it should."

CHAPTER 2: WHAT IS CLIMATE CHANGE?

I am not going into this book with any preconceived notions about what you may or may not know. My years as a teacher demonstrated that assuming a class knows anything the moment you walk in the door is a dangerous one. If you think you know the basics of climate change, you're under no obligation at all to read this chapter. Skip ahead.

On the other hand, if you don't know very much—or if you know something but would benefit from a refresher—don't feel at all self-conscious. Settle down and get comfortable, and we'll have you up to speed forthwith.

Climate change is, simply put, when the climate of Earth, or any part of it, changes for any reason. Climates can get warmer or cooler, more or less rainy or snowy, and they can be mild or severe. When we talk about climate change we could be talking about the climate of the whole Earth, or the climate of Wauwatosa, Wisconsin. The terms "global warming" and "climate change" are not synonymous—I'll get to that in a moment—but they sometimes (not always) refer to the same phenomenon.

Here's a helpful place to start.

What Is Climate? What Is Weather?

Look up from this book and look outside your window. Whatever it's doing out there: that's weather. The app I check on my phone every morning to see if it's going to rain today or what coat I should bring when I leave the house: that's weather.

The best way to describe the difference between weather and climate is to liken it to a difference between a person's behavior, and their character. I may do a good deed today. I might help an old lady cross the street or I might give $100 to the Native American College Fund. That's *behavior*. I may have done these generous things. But if I'm doing those things a lot—if I'm starting foundations and devoting my life to good deeds, if I do so many good deeds so regularly and so fundamentally that I'm being compared to Mother Teresa—people might start to say that I'm a generous person. That would be my *character*.

It works that way with weather and climate. We think of Miami as having a hot, humid climate. That doesn't mean that tomorrow it might not be cloudy and dry with a high temperature of 58 degrees. But if it was like that in Miami a lot, especially in the summer, we would begin to think differently about Miami's climate. Just as a generous, good-natured person could do something petty or unkind now and again—even Mother Teresa had her bad days—the weather of a place might be out of sync with its climate.

Incidentally, this is why a cold day in a warm place, or a snowstorm, doesn't "disprove" global warming. (Sometimes heavy snowfalls are actually evidence of man-made climate change, but that's a different issue). Many denialist arguments about climate change seek deliberately to confuse people about the difference between weather and climate. They're not the same.

Are "Climate Change" and "Global Warming" The Same Thing?

No. Despite the common usage of these terms as interchangeable—or denialists' false arguments that "They changed the name for political reasons!"—they don't mean the same thing, and the terms have been used for decades. Climate may change on a scale that isn't worldwide, and it may change in the direction of cooling, not warming. See some examples in the "Has It Happened Before?" section, below.

"Global warming" is a type of climate change, but not all climate change is global warming. All Impalas are Chevrolets, but not all Chevrolets are Impalas. It just so happens that our modem episode of climate change—the one that's been caused mostly by industrial activity and the burning of fossil fuels since the late 18th century—*is* global warming. Because it is caused mainly by humans, sometimes it is called "anthropogenic global warming," or AGW. "Anthropogenic," with its Greek root word *anthro-* meaning man or humans, is a descriptor that indicates where this particular type of climate change comes from.

So Why Is The Earth's Climate Getting Warmer?

Here's the science part. Some gases, due to their physical and molecular properties, absorb heat when they're in the atmosphere. Carbon dioxide, the principal by-product of the burning of fossil fuels, happens to be one of these gases. So is methane, which may be naturally-occurring, or caused (or released) by human processes. The more of this stuff we have in the atmosphere, the more heat the atmosphere traps and prevents from radiating off into space. It's that simple.

The fact that gases have these properties is, in the abstract, a good thing. If they didn't, the Earth's surface would be too cold to support life. The problem is that now, in the last 250 years, we've got much more of these heat trapping gases than we need and they're becoming a huge problem. Once a molecule of carbon dioxide rises into the atmosphere or is absorbed by the oceans, it sends to stay there for a long time. It's highly possible that much of the CO_2 that came from the first puff of exhaust from the first experimental internal combustion engine, created by Gottlieb Daimler in the 1870s, is still floating around up there or has been absorbed by the ocean. You may have just inhaled a molecule or two of CO_2 from that puff of exhaust with your last breath; a molecule from that puff of exhaust may have slid past your toe the last time you walked barefoot on the beach.

Has It Happened Before?

Which one, climate change or global warming? Actually that's a trick question. Yes, both have happened before—but neither have happened within the realm of recorded human history on the same scale that they're happening now. So, in short, yes, it's happened before, but that turns out to not be a very comforting answer.

There have been several episodes of global warming in the Earth's past. Most are in the very distant past, hundreds of millions of years. Obviously they were not caused by the burning of fossil fuels, but they have been linked to large-scale increases in greenhouse gases. About 252 million years ago, an extremely depressing thing happened that has come to be known as the Permian-Triassic Extinction Event. Its cause might have been a huge volcanic event known as the "Siberian Traps" which may have had the effect of releasing a lot of methane into the atmosphere, but we're not sure. What we do know is that between 70% and 96% of all species then on Earth died out over the next few hundred thousand years. This is one of five past events of major extinctions.

The sixth such major extinction is happening now. And yes, it's linked to climate change, our modern episode of global warming.

I don't need to tell you what happened to the dino-saurs. That event, known as the K-T Event, happened about 65,000,000 years ago, and it's why you've never eaten a brontosaurus steak or seen a T-Rex outside of a movie. The asteroid hypothesis has been around since 1980, considerably lesser time than we have known about man-made global warming. But dinosaurs are def-initely not a thing anymore, probably as a result of some kind of climate change perhaps with a very sudden and catastrophic cause.

This kind of thing may have happened more recently. About 75,000 years ago, when most humans looked like those ape people in the New York City Museum of Natu-ral History's dioramas, a volcano called Toba erupted and shrouded the Earth in a veil of volcanic dust. In 1998, some anthropologists noted that the genetic diver-sity of human beings is much less than it would be if the human species had propagated in linear fashion from the East African rift valleys where our collective history began, and they suggested that the Toba eruption killed as much as 90% of the human beings then living on Earth. This theory is controversial and has not been ac-corded the same mantle of being an "extinction event" as the Permian-Triassic or K-T Events; the theory was hot (no pun intended) in some academic circles about a decade ago but seems to have cooled off since then. But if it happened, it would mean that most of us are the progeny of the few huddled survivors of the Toba Catas-trophe. Somehow we found a way to survive.

Much more recently, in the decade of the 1810s, something similar to the Toba Catastrophe scenario repeated itself on a much smaller scale. Two volcanoes, one we haven't identified and the other called Tambora, erupted in February 1809 and April 1815, respectively, and also pumped a bunch of volcanic crap into the stratosphere. The results caused it to snow in Boston in June and triggered food riots in Switzerland. They also helped drive the retired President Thomas Jefferson further into penury. By 1820 the world recovered, but this episode of climate change—global cooling instead of global warming—was the last that we experienced before we began to burn fossil fuels on a large scale, and it was the last episode of worldwide climate change that arose from natural causes.

There's much more that can be said about the long history of climate change. But let's move on, and tackle some more questions that may be on your mind.

CHAPTER 3: IS IT REAL?

The way the media has traditionally covered climate change, you could be forgiven for thinking that there's some sort of legitimate controversy about the causes and existence of global warming. There isn't, but the media, and certain other interests, have deliberately tried to make it into a horse race. The science is settled: climate change is happening, and human beings and their activities are the major cause. If 99 doctors told you that you had cancer and needed an operation immediately, and one told you that there was nothing to worry about, unless you were deluded or suicidal you would definitely be persuaded by the 99.

Usually at this point, someone talking about climate change, in refuting the denialist position, would fall back on scientific data to prove their point. I'm not going to do that, because the science that proves the reality and causation of global warming is ubiquitous and easily accessed and it needs no cheerleading from me. No one's hiding it. The scientific case for climate change and its causation is literally overwhelming. It's clearly the *best* case in favor, but it's been so well-established that I don't think I need to rehash it here.

Instead, I will fall back on my role as a lawyer—yes, I practiced law for many years—to bring you additional evidentiary arguments that, even *independently* of the well-settled science, demonstrate beyond any doubt that climate change is real, and that denialism is a crock.

In the past ten years, many lawsuits have been filed in numerous courts in the United States and around the world. In the U.S., the most famous one so far is *Juliana v. United States*, the "climate kids" who sued the federal government for causing climate change. I was, for a time, a consultant on this case, albeit in a minor role. But there are many, many other such cases. Governmental entities, agencies and oil companies have been sued over climate change on numerous theories, and the tide of litigation is steadily rising. The oil companies themselves have long expected—and feared—that they'll soon be on the business end of crippling liability payouts for damages related to climate change, which is why investing in fossil fuel stocks is a bad idea.

In any event, in all of these cases, not a single defendant has ever argued in open court that climate change is not happening or that humans are not the main cause of it. Indeed, in *Juliana*, the government—the same one headed by a politician known for his denialism—stipulated, on the record, that they agreed that climate change is real and is caused by humans.

From a standpoint of legal strategy, this is conclusive that denialist arguments have no factual validity. If there really *was* a factual basis to doubt the reality or causation of climate change, the first defendant who was ever sued in a U.S. court would have been eager to take the case to trial so as to get on record, in front of a jury, the factual case against climate change or human causation. If the facts proven in open court showed that climate change was questionable, and a jury or judge so found, that case would quickly have become a legal precedent that would need only to be cited in a brief supporting a motion to dismiss in order to dispose of most, if not all, subsequent climate change cases. In other words, if the reality of climate change really was factually questionable, a courtroom would be the place to show it, and it would be a magic bullet for anyone else ever accused of climate-related malfeasance.

Why, if climate change isn't real, would the U.S. government, ExxonMobil, numerous other foreign countries, states, provinces and corporations pretend to agree that it was, thus limiting their route of escape from potentially ruinous legal results to a much narrower path, if they had a magic bullet they could reach for that would conclusively exonerate them for all time?

Another clue that denialism is fake is how quickly and suddenly it arose—and from what quarters. Denialism wasn't really a thing before the late 1980s. A great deal of scientific work was done during that decade, particularly with computerized climate modeling. The early 1980s saw the development of new computing technology that made more detailed modeling possible in a way it hadn't been before. Before the 1980s, the existence and causation of global warming was generally uncontroversial. It was a question of nailing down the accuracy of what was already known and projected, not the basics of understanding whether climate change was happening and what was causing it. But suddenly in the late 1980s, material questioning the reality of climate change began leaking out of industry groups and think tanks funded by conservatives and the fossil fuel lobby. Looking back on it, it's very easy to see that denial or doubt about climate change did not arise organically or spontaneously. It was a coordinated public relations and lobbying campaign.

This is proven beyond all doubt by documents from oil giant ExxonMobil that leaked in 2015. After Exxon's own in-house scientists thoroughly studied climate change in the 1970s and concluded that it was a major threat to the fossil fuel industry, quite suddenly in the 1990s—about the time the Kyoto Protocol was being negotiated—documents show that Exxon deliberately sought to mislead the public on the reality of climate change. And it's not just ExxonMobil; similar documents have been uncovered implicating Shell in the same scandal. In an infamous 1997 memo, the American Petroleum Institute, heavily funded by Exxon and other oil giants stated bluntly, "Victory will be achieved when...those promoting the Kyoto treaty on the basis of extant science appear to be out of touch with reality." Does that sound like rational doubt to you?

Finally, consider the people who are most vulnerable to climate change and where they live. Small island nations like Vanuatu or the Maldives will be among the first countries where significant chunks of their real estate will disappear due to sea level rise. These nations are already suffering the effects of intensified weather disasters like typhoons and cyclones, and they're already preparing plans to move their populations elsewhere. These are among the poorest countries on Earth. They lack the resources to deal with this existential problem. If climate change was so easily disproven by deniers' arguments, wouldn't these countries jump at the chance to not have to devote significant portions of their small national wealth to dealing with a problem that turns out to be fake? If you were the Prime Minister of Vanuatu, wouldn't "global warming isn't happening after all" be the most welcome news you could ever hear? Yet somehow the leaders and citizens of these at-risk nations are taking climate change very seriously.

The arguments I've made in this chapter, remember, are outside of the scientific data that already proves, beyond all doubt, that climate change is happening and is caused by human beings. The body of scientific work that establishes this is mammoth, exhaustive and public.

That alone should convince any rational person of the reality and the human causation of climate change—and it does convince the vast majority of people around the world. But in case that body of data needs any more reinforcing, the points I've made here, which are evidentiary in nature, are absolutely consistent with the scientific data.

Climate change is real. It just is. Let's move on.

CHAPTER 4: HOW DID WE FIND OUT ABOUT IT?

When I first began speaking publicly about climate change, the earliest talks I gave were centered around its history—how scientists discovered that the Earth was warming, and how they figured out what was causing it. Most of the audiences I spoke to knew almost nothing of this story. Many people assume that because climate change has only been on the public radar for the last few decades that it must have been discovered fairly recently. Actually, we've known about it for more than a century. If that surprises you, you're not alone.

The discovery of global warming was not a "Eureka!" moment in the history of science, like the oft-repeated legend (probably untrue) about an apple falling on Isaac Newton's head and causing him to discover gravity. In the real world, scientific discovery rarely works like that. Instead, scientists build incrementally on previous discoveries, slowly pushing the envelope of knowledge a little at a time. That's what happened with climate change,

The idea that climate could change, and that it could do so as a result of human activity, goes back more than 200 years. Thomas Jefferson, for example, wrote about man-made climate change in *Notes on the State of Virginia*, published in 1786. He observed that the winters in Virginia were slightly warmer and shorter at that time than they had been in early Colonial days, because deforestation, cultivation and development had altered the climate of the New World. Carbon dioxide and the greenhouse effect were nowhere in Jefferson's thinking—which was, incidentally, shared by many naturalists of the period—but at its root this was a theory of anthropogenic climate change. Jefferson obsessively took weather readings and recorded them over a period of many years, in part, to build a body of data to prove his suppositions on climate change. If Jefferson took a ride in Marty McFly's Delorean time machine and ended up in our own era, I doubt he'd be surprised that our climate is now much warmer than it was in 1786.

In 1856 a scientist from Goshen, Connecticut, Eunice Newton Foote, conducted a series of studies on the radiative properties of gases. She discovered that what they called at that time "carbonic acid"—carbon dioxide—absorbed heat more than other atmospheric gases did. Three years later Irish-born scientist John Tyndall conducted a similar experiment and got the same result. In 1896, Svante Arrhenius, a Swedish electrochemist, made calculations of likely changes in the Earth's surface temperature based on changes to the carbon dioxide content of the atmosphere. Together, we can credit Foote and Arrhenius with discovering the greenhouse effect.

Arrhenius also linked the greenhouse effect to the burning of fossil fuel. He wrote in 1908 that an increase in CO_2 content of the atmosphere, as a result of the burning of carbon-based fuels in industrial processes, would manifest itself as global warming. In 1908 this was a theory, but over the next several decades empirical observations of temperature and CO_2 took the theory into the realm of proven fact. In 1938 a British scientist, Guy Callendar, made an estimate of the amount of CO_2 that had gone into the atmosphere since roughly 1870. Beginning in 1958, measurements of atmospheric CO_2— the famous "Keeling Curve"—showed that Callendar's estimates were right-on. And as reliable weather data taken in systematic fashion began to emerge at the end of the 19th century, it showed that temperature trends were rising exactly in tandem with carbon dioxide— exactly as Arrhenius had predicted years before.

The congruence of mean temperatures with the increase in CO_2 is the unmistakable human fingerprint on climate change. Scientists predicted as far back as 1896 that this is exactly what we'd see once we had all the data in hand. Certainly by the 1960s we *had* the data, and we saw exactly what Arrhenius, Callendar and others predicted we'd see. The hypothesis was proven. Climate change exists, and we're causing most of it.

Since the 1960s, most scientific analysis of climate change has not been focused on questions of, "Is it happening?" or "What's causing it?", but rather, "How fast is it moving?" and "What are the effects going to be?" What was usually then referred to as "the greenhouse effect" or "the CO_2 problem" began to hit the public and policy radar about that time. President Lyndon Johnson was briefed on climate change in 1965; a White House report on the quality of the environment specifically mentioned the threat of global warming. The first references to human-caused climate change appear in Congressional hearings testimony earlier than that, in 1957. The documents, which are all public, clearly show that the U.S. government has known about the problems of climate change since the Eisenhower administration.

Unfortunately, throughout the 1970s and 1980s, the issue of climate change was always something that was off in the future, and rarely seen as a clear and present danger. The "How fast is it moving?" question inevitably morphed into a more ominous one, "How quickly do we have to change course in order to avoid the worst effects?" Whenever this question was studied, the answer was usually "Very soon." In 1983, for example, a U.S. Environmental Protection Agency report on climate change made quiet ripples in the national press, especially when its author, Robert M, White, President of the National Academy of Engineering, stated that we had 10 to 20 years to study the problem, but then we'd better be ready to change policy—meaning to curb our society's reliance on fossil fuels. White's deadline ran out in 2003.

Climate change really entered the public consciousness at the end of the 1980s. What was then the worst drought in American history since the Depression era punished and withered farm fields across the nation in 1988, the same summer that climate scientist James Hansen testified before the Senate that "global warming has begun." That same year saw the formation of the United Nations' Intergovernmental Panel on Climate Change, which undertook the task of studying and synthesizing all extant scientific literature around the world on the subject of climate change.

The IPCC's first report on climate change, which came out in 1990, ranks right up there with the U.N. Charter on Human Rights, "I Have a Dream" and James Joyce's *Ulysses* as one of the most important documents of the entire 20th century. It laid out carefully what was known about climate change (a lot), and what its effects might be (most of them not very pleasant). The IPCC has since made several more reports, the latest one released in October 2018. The trajectory and evolution of the IPCC's projections on the effects of climate change has been remarkably consistent: it's moving much faster, and pinching harder, than ever predicted. One thing you never hear from a climate scientist is, "Gee, *that* took longer to happen than I thought it would."

You'll notice there's a name missing from this brief history of climate change that most people expect to see: Al Gore. In reality he's a pretty minor player in the history of climate change. The former Vice-President's documentary film *An Inconvenient Truth* from 2006 did raise awareness on climate change, but Gore, who was out of national power long before he made the film, is not the source of any previously unknown insights on climate change. If anything, Gore's visibility on the issue may have made it harder to deal with the problem, as his status as a political lightning rod may have had a lot to do with the hardening of one side of the American political spectrum against even taking climate change seriously. In my view, climate change has been ill-served by many of those who worked hardest to publicize it. The ubiquitous image of a doleful-looking polar bear on a melting ice floe—which reinforces the message that climate change is a distant problem happening far away and threatening animals but not humans—is an unfortunate example.

This very brief history is necessarily truncated and oversimplified. Many more people, events and phenomena wrapped up in the history of climate change deserve to be talked about, from T.C. Chamberlin and Roger Revelle and their role in discovering the carbon cycle and how CO_2 affects the oceans, to Michael Mann's famous "hockey stick" graph and its status as a flash point for denialists. But this is the basic, bare-bones story of how we found out about climate change. This is largely a story about scientific discovery and how it found its way into politics and policy. But while all this was going on, tailpipes were puffing, factory smokestacks smoking, and ice slowly melting all over the world. Let's turn in the next chapter to that very different kind of history.

CHAPTER 5: WHEN DID IT START?

I've already talked about previous episodes of changes in the Earth's climate in Chapter 2. Now let's talk about the episode of climate change we're in right now: anthropogenic global warming, caused mostly by human activity, principally industrial processes.

Through the mechanism of industrialization—and specifically its chief power source of fossil fuels—climate change has historically been linked to energy usage. For all but the last tiny sliver of time, humanity has generally not used a lot of energy. The vast majority of energy we've used in any enterprise, from building the Pyramids of Giza to fighting the Napoleonic Wars, has been animal in nature, and by "animal" I specifically include humans. Most farm fields in world history have been plowed by humans, horses, oxen or some combination thereof. Horses pulled chariots in ancient Rome and fashionable buggies through Central Park in New York eighteen centuries later. Chemical energy, like the fire in a blacksmith's hearth or small early steamboats in American waters in the first decades of the 19th century, was a factor, but it was usually powered by burning wood. Coal was mined in China, the pre-Colombian Americas and the Roman Empire, and coal mines existed throughout the Middle Ages, but coal was a minor player for most of this time and mining operations were small-scale compared to what they'd eventually become.

The 19th century greatly changed human beings' relationship to energy. The stirrings of industrialization stretch back to the Enlightenment, when a scientific revolution occurred in rough tandem with western European philosophers' development of ideas about economics—think Adam Smith's *Wealth of Nations*—and the ideology of liberalism. I mean "liberalism" here in its historical sense, as a democratic order that was an alternative to monarchism, not in its modern context of a liberal vs. conservative political spectrum. These developments were important. The scientific revolution taught us how to make stuff; the economic ideas of the Enlightenment enabled us to figure out how to pay for the making of stuff on a mass scale; and the political ideas that gave rise to modern capitalist democracies made the making of stuff (and the making of money from the making of stuff) not only possible and desirable, but actually incentivized. These vast stuff-making enterprises would take an awful lot of energy. Where was it going to come from?

At first, the Industrial Revolution was at least theoretically renewable. The earliest large-scale factories, which usually made textiles especially in Britain and the United States, were powered by water, which explains why they were located on rivers. But there's only so many rivers to go around, and those that were used to power factories quickly became polluted. Coal proved a much better—and much more portable—power source. The British especially loved coal, and quickly adopted it not merely to drive factories but for everyday use such as in home fireplaces. If you're in London, you can quickly tell which buildings were there during the early Victorian age: they're the ones permanently streaked with gray from the decades of rain infused with coal dust from the city's chimneys. St. Paul's Cathedral, consecrated in 1697 and which used to be white in color, is an example.

This was all going on while another revolution, this one involving interior illumination, was also occurring. The world was a very dark place before the mid-19th century, with candles deployed in some form being the main way to see your hand in front of your face on a dark night. Whale oil, like coal something long-known but comparatively little-used, quite suddenly became big business in the early 19th century. If there was ever a business that was the opposite of sustainability, the whale oil business was it. With fleets of *Pequods* and Captain Ahabs scouring the oceans for that magic stuff to light the parlors of Boston and Paris, the world whale population nose-dived. We should have learned a lesson from this, but, predictably, we didn't.

Then came the alpha and the omega of all fossil fuels: petroleum. Oil did not immediately become the central fuel of our civilization. It took a while. Between 1859, when the first commercial oil well was sunk in western Pennsylvania, to the end of the century, when cars started to appear, petroleum was part of that lucrative interior illumination market. Kerosene was the main product. John D. Rockefeller's Standard Oil, the octopus that gave birth to many of our modern oil companies such as ExxonMobil and Chevron, was established in 1870 to market kerosene for lamps. What few whales were still alive in 1870 might have welcomed the respite, but this is about when our climate problems began. In 1949 Guy Callendar (remember him?) estimated that the CO_2 content of the atmosphere was about 290 ppm (parts per million) in the year Standard Oil came into being. It's been going up ever since.

The development of the automobile exploded the market for oil companies' products. At least in dense urban environments, horses were already being phased out at the end of the 19th century, usually in favor of electric vehicles like Boston's famous trolleys. The internal combustion engine, however, could conquer both urban and rural transportation challenges, and enterprising fellows like Henry Ford figured out how to make them affordable to average people. Oil also proved its worth in the chief human endeavor of the 20th century, that being war. Tanks plowing through the mud of the Western Front and rickety biplanes buzzing around over it during World War I were both inventive—and deadly— uses of petroleum. A second world war a few decades later would be about petroleum to a significant degree: the Japanese attacked Pearl Harbor in 1941, for example, as part of a multi-pronged strategy to gain access to rich oil fields of the Dutch East Indies. Even the trigger for that attack was based on oil: the Japanese decided on war only after the United States ceased exporting oil to Japan. The Japanese needed it to continue their war in China.

During these two centuries, the 19th and especially the 20th, humanity plugged into the hidden battery that had been hidden under the Earth and milked it for all it was worth. You have to admit that we did some pretty clever things with petroleum, and not just in engines. We defeated Hitler, built the interstate highway system, put men on the Moon, and knitted the world together with communications technology, all directly or indirectly as a result of energy and materials derived principally from petroleum. But we also fouled the oceans with pollution, especially petroleum-based plastics, and punched that CO_2-ppm meter ever higher.

If one takes a long view, the sudden explosive burst of energy and activity that's occurred since 1800 is very much an aberration in the course of human history. We haven't lived with technology above the medieval level for very much of our collective existence on this planet. We like our new toys, but they're very much still new to us, and we haven't figured out quite how to use them safely. A period of adjustment is obviously what follows, and the chief value that must govern during that adjustment is not greed, but wisdom.

During this brief history of climate change, something else happened that I think is quite relevant and instructive. In 1945, the human species developed nuclear weapons. They were used twice in anger and then, since 1945, mainly as a bluff, a theoretical instrument to deter, frighten, coerce or bargain away. (South Africa gave up its nukes voluntarily in 1989 in part as a bargaining chip to mollify a world outraged at its apartheid policies). The very real danger of nuclear destruction seems to have served as a wake-up call for world leaders, especially at the end of the 1980s. The nuclear threat is by no means ended, but far fewer people today expect civilization to end in a nuclear exchange between superpowers than did in 1985, where such a result was believed by many to be inevitable.

What happened in the case of nukes? The decision to launch a nuclear war and thus annihilate humanity was, and remains, exclusively under the control of a very small group of people. Those people, as a group, eventually realized that there was no political objective worth achieving at the cost of destroying human civilization. That's not to say that a madman couldn't someday press a nuclear button, but, for now at least, no member of the small group with control over nuclear weapons has concluded that launching an atomic holocaust is a rational choice. It was only ever a small group of people who needed to be convinced, and that made all the difference.

The majority of greenhouse gas emissions that are causing climate change are, like nuclear weapons, under the control of a relatively small group of people. If only a few major companies or industries changed their behavior, we would take a huge chunk out of climate change, and the others would follow. If a small group of political leaders recognized that there was no political objective worth achieving at the cost of a nuclear war, is it so far-fetched to believe that a small group of economic leaders might ultimately recognize that there is no *economic* objective worth achieving at the cost of runaway climate change?

Hope in the face of climate change is not just wishful thinking. It has historical precedent. That's not a bad place to start.

CHAPTER 6: WHAT CAN WE EXPECT?

This is the big question, isn't it? What is a climate-changed world going to be like? A lot of people are expending a great deal of effort to try to answer this question. It's also a dangerous question, because what we do to address climate change largely depends on the answer. It's always dangerous to prognosticate, but that doesn't mean that we don't have at least *some* clear ideas on what we can expect.

We're on the safest ground, speaking in terms of accuracy, at predicting that certain things that have already happened as a result of climate change are going to keep happening, and will probably happen more often. The years 2017 and 2018, especially 2018, were major milestones in public awareness of climate change, and the real factor that seems to get people's attention is their lived experience. Most of us didn't have to read scientific journals to know how miserable the summer of 2018 was in the northern hemisphere and 2018-19 was in the southern. Most of us lived through it. It wasn't just what we ourselves experienced, but observing extreme weather events like hurricanes and wildfires made many people take notice of the climate change problem. Hurricane Katrina was an eye-opener in 2005, nearly fifteen years ago. Now we have more than one Katrina every summer, somewhere in the world, and people are noticing it. It's safe to say that we're going to have more extreme weather events in the future.

We can also be pretty confident in predictions that scientists have made with remarkable unanimity, and which are backed by things that have already happened. I'm not aware of a single scientist who doesn't think sea levels will rise, by some significant amount, over the next few years and decades. Rising tides aren't just a function of melting ice at the poles, either. Much of the sea level rise we expect comes from thermal expansion—warmer water takes up more space than cold water does. This, again, comports with lived experience. The first time I saw water rising in streets and alleyways in Miami Beach—what Floridians call "sunny day flooding"—I suddenly understood sea level rise in a much more tangible way.

Sea level rise is a big deal. If you think an inch of sea level rise doesn't sound like much, think about how you'd react if you found an inch of water in your basement. The sea may rise by as much as five feet in New York City by the end of the century. That by no means heralds the end of New York City, but it does mean that a great deal of engineering, rebuilding or relocating is going to have to be done to a great many parts of it. The economic resources and political will probably exist to do this kind of job on the Big Apple, but what about low-lying, densely-packed coastal cities in Africa or Bangladesh, or Pacific and Indian Ocean island nations? The people who live there now are going to have to move, eventually. Sea level rise is going to trigger mass migrations of people.

This prediction, again, jives with what we know has already happened. We have already seen that events related to climate change have the potential to spark mass migrations. Let's take the example of Hurricane Katrina again. The intensity of the hurricane was most likely an effect of climate change. (Asking whether a particular hurricane was "caused" by climate change is an absurd question; it's like asking how many of Barry Bonds's home runs were "caused" by him abusing steroids). Katrina triggered what may have been the largest internal migration of people within the United States—most of them African-Americans—since the Great Depression. Many thousands displaced from the New Orleans area never returned and population was slow to recover. This has *already* happened, and in the United States, not the developing world. Further effects of climate change will undoubtedly cause population migrations.

Other effects of climate change are likely. Among the most disturbing findings of what is happening involves animals and species extinction. I already mentioned that we are now experiencing the sixth major extinction event in Earth's history, the Permian-Triassic Extinction Event being the largest. Reading about species extinction is where you really need to keep FDR's "fear itself" line ringing in your head.

It is fact that species are going extinct at an alarming rate, much faster than the average in history before humans began reengineering the planet on a large scale. Both aquatic species and insects appear to be suffering greatly from climate change, and from other effects like overfishing or cultivation of spaces that were previously wild, such as in the Amazon region. Insects and marine invertebrates are at the bottom of the food webs on land and ocean, respectively. If their biodiversity continues to decline as it has been doing, the effects on the planet—and on human food supplies—could be catastrophic. Obviously that has not happened yet, but it's at least possible, perhaps likely, based on what has been observed to have happened so far.

Disease is another depressing potential effect of climate change. As the Earth warms, the hydrological cycle—how water moves through the oceans, lands and the atmosphere—speeds up, which is part of why climate change produces more and greater droughts, higher floods and other extreme weather events. All of these effects stir up reservoirs of infectious diseases that were previously at rest, or mostly at rest. Furthermore, the kind of human activity that causes climate change—like resource exploitation in formerly wild areas—brings humans into closer contact with diseases that were previously not very likely to spread to human populations, or at least not as easily. Thus, humans are increasingly at risk of infectious disease outbreaks as a result of climate change.

These predictions are consistent with historical experience. One can argue whether the emergence of HIV/AIDS is legitimately linked to climate change, but it's undeniable that its emergence is connected to human activity in much the same way that scientists predict future diseases will be. The history of HIV is complicated and hard to pin down, but it seems to have originally circulated in primates in equatorial Africa, and then made the jump to humans in the late 19th or more likely early 20th century. That was exactly the same time that European countries were intensively extracting resources from Africa during their grand colonialism projects that preceded the two world wars. Indeed, the common genetic ancestor of most HIV infections appears to have first appeared in Leopoldville (now Kinshasa), the capital of the Belgian Congo, in the 1920s. Colonialism got HIV into the human bloodstream, and globalization spread it. The emergence of Ebola follows a similar pattern, although it is much more lethal than AIDS and thus harder to spread into a truly global pandemic. But the point is that the predictions of the disease effects of climate change are plausible given what has already happened.

One thing we *cannot* expect is for climate change to reverse itself anytime soon—at least not in our lifetimes, or our children's, or our children's children's lifetimes. The number one denialist argument against climate change is, "Climate has changed before," as if we could wake up tomorrow and find temperatures declining, sea level going back down and species extinction reversing itself. Climate *has* changed before, but once changed on the scale that we've changed it with the burning of fossil fuels, it takes a *long* time—tens or even hundreds of thousands of years—to return to its former condition. We know this from the study of past geologic eras. Only comparatively minor climate changes, like the Cold Decade of the 1810s, return to "normal" within human life spans. Looking at it through the lens of human experience, climate change is, for us and the next few generations, definitely a permanent condition.

That said, it is not time to throw in the towel. It's not hopeless, we're not screwed, and we shouldn't choose to lay down and die. It's not, as I said in the introduction, "the end of history." Climate change presents challenges to our society and our species. We have no choice but to adapt to those challenges. It also presents opportunities. About those, we *do* have a choice. Dealing with challenges is mandatory. Seizing opportunities is optional.

Putting fear and defeatism aside, let us take a reasoned look, through the magic glasses of history, and make some educated guesses about what is ending in the era of climate change—and what's beginning. Some of what's coming may surprise you.

CHAPTER 7: WHAT IS ENDING?

As one era of human history closes and another one opens, by definition many things will end. Nothing lasts forever. Everyone knows that logically and instinctively, but it's amazing how often we act as if certain things in our lives are permanent. This has been a particularly dangerous way of thinking in the decades and centuries that have led up to our present predicament.

In a way, it's all about time scale. When I talk to businesspeople, I sometimes remind them that certain things—even things we regard as the bedrocks of our society and the business world—will eventually end. Let's take just one example: the New York Stock Exchange. Many people in business begin their day by checking what "the market" is doing, up or down. Most of the time they're talking about the Dow Jones Industrial Average, still the best-known of the market averages. It's one of the pillars of the financial community and the world economy. The NYSE was founded in 1792, and the DJIA has existed since February 16, 1885. And someday, as a result of some circumstances we do not yet know, the New York Stock Exchange will cease to exist. This means that some day coming in the future will be the very last day on which this venerable institution remains in operation. Possibly it will change form and morph into something else, but that something else will eventually end too. It's 100% guaranteed that, in some form, there will be a final bell, a last quote, an ultimate close that will not be followed by an opening the next day. Somebody out there will eventually buy the very last share of any company ever traded on the NYSE.

We understand this in the abstract. But most of us, when confronted with the abstract idea of a "permanent" institution like the NYSE coming to an end, absolve ourselves of having to think about it by concluding, "Yes, but it's highly unlikely it would ever happen in my lifetime." If you think that, chances are very good you're right; the last time there was *not* a New York Stock Exchange, the French Revolution was still going on. But there's also a chance—however small—that you're wrong. The NYSE might indeed end in your lifetime. What would happen, how would your life or that of your business, change if it did?

History can confound expectations. John F. Kennedy was the youngest man elected President of the United States when he narrowly won the 1960 election. Although he suffered from severe health issues, kept mostly secret from the public, it was still quite likely—and widely expected—that the Kennedy presidency would continue until at least 1965, if not 1969 assuming he was reelected to a second term. The tragedy in Dallas on November 22, 1963 was so shocking in part because it was so unexpected. History does sometimes work this way.

Here's another thought experiment we can use to explore the dimensions of historical change. Make a list of 50 specific institutions or organizations in the world today that you believe are more or less permanent—that you cannot imagine ending in your lifetime, or at least not any time soon. They should be easy to think of: the Catholic Church, the United States Constitution, the Internal Revenue Service, the British royal family, the Chinese Communist Party, Lloyd's of London insurance company, what-have-you. Although it's impossible to figure events of history according to mathematical averages, consider your list of 50 permanent institutions and then imagine that you are wrong—just for the sake of argument—about the permanence or stability of ten percent of them. Take your pen and cross five entries, chosen at random, off your list. Now imagine what the world is like without those institutions, and try to do so with an open mind, meaning, without assigning a probability judgment to them, or dismissing the idea with a flip, "That could never happen." What kind of world are you looking at on your page? Probably one you had never thought of before.

As interesting as this is, don't draw the wrong lesson from this exercise: I'm not arguing that history is essentially random. It isn't. But what I *am* saying is that the stability and permanence of institutions are very often overestimated, and that we tend to assume the world as it is now is the way it will likely be, for the most part, throughout our lifetimes. I can predict with a high degree of certainty that *some* course that history takes over the remainder of your lifetime *will* surprise you.

What I hope to do in the next two chapters—which are lengthy, and thus broken into sub-chapters—is to take a little bit of the surprise out of the future that climate change and other processes are making for us. We *can* make educated guesses about what's coming. This is not "predicting the future" in the tea-leaves, crystal ball sense. Instead it is more like historical thinking projected forward. As a historian I know something about the factors at play in the fall of the Western Roman Empire, and I may know enough about them to make an argument about why that event happened. Here, I can make arguments based on educated consideration of the facts about what may be in store. It is the process of thinking about these issues, not the ultimate validation of a "prediction," that is valuable here.

So what, in our world of today, is *ending* as a result of climate change and the various other changes it is driving?

CHAPTER 7.1: ENDING: THE POST-WORLD WAR II ORDER

At least compared to the last couple of centuries before it, the world has, with some notable exceptions, been remarkably stable in the decades since the end of the Second World War in 1945. There have been no major wars between superpowers, and despite rapid changes in technology, human society has not undergone any radical shifts.

That world is ending. Or perhaps it is even accurate to say that it *has ended*, past tense.

To understand how and why the post-World War II political and economic order is ending, we first have to understand what it was and how we got it. The Second World War was undoubtedly a great upheaval with far-reaching consequences. As a historian I am less convinced by what one might term the ideological interpretation of World War II, that being a struggle of fascism versus freedom. (If that's really what World War II was about, how come the Soviet Union, one of the most unfree countries in the world at that time, was on our side?) I believe it is more accurately viewed as an attempt by two powers, Hitler's Germany and militarist-fascist Japan, to knock the colonial powers—Britain, France, Holland and the United States—off the top of the food chain of world resources. Essentially, Hitler and the Japanese saw the other powers dining at a lavish banquet table, and they thought, "*We* should have a seat at that table, and *they've* been there long enough." Their attempt ultimately failed, but the long banquet certainly *was* interrupted; dinner wasn't quite the same after that. This was why, in the years after the war, Britain lost most of her empire, the U.S. gave up the Philippines, and the French were kicked out of Algeria and Indochina.

World War II has a lot to do with climate change, and that nexus especially concerns the United States. In order to win the war, the U.S. had to build out its huge industrial capacity which enabled us to churn out positively gargantuan quantities of stuff: bombers, Jeeps, tanks, Liberty ships, and, toward the end, a couple of atomic bombs. The war and its economic stimulus ended the Great Depression, and after 1945 political and economic leaders were determined *not* to have a post-war slump. Thus, America's new industrial capacity kept right on operating at full tilt, but instead of making planes and tanks, it started making consumer goods like cars, lawnmowers and television sets, and just about anything else you could think of. The rise of a consumerist society following World War II is largely responsible for the disposable, petroleum-driven culture that has gotten us into such a fix on climate change. It's not solely Americans' fault, but after 1945, being like the United

States, and living at the high standards of Americans, became attractive to many people around the world.

The post-World War II order also has a political component. Beginning in the late 1940s the world was carved into two hostile camps, Western democracies and the Soviet bloc. But even through that process, European countries sought to bring themselves closer together, economically and politically, to serve as a sort of counterbalance to the two superpowers. That's how the European Union came into being. Particularly since the 1980s, political and economic leaders advocating globalization have essentially been working on a similar project: ensure the political stability of the world by binding the world's major economies so tightly together that a major war among them would be economically unthinkable.

Finally, we have to say something about nuclear weapons. The atom bomb has been used only twice in anger, both times by the United States against Japan in the closing days of the war. Since then, the main utility of nukes has been psychological and theoretical: scare your enemies into not attacking you for fear of devastating retaliation. As frightening as they are, and as close as the world has come to nuclear holocaust—during the Cuban Missile Crisis in 1962 and the Soviet false launch detection incident of 1983—there's a case to be made, however imperfectly, that nuclear weapons have had a stabilizing effect on international politics. And, as I mentioned earlier, the decision not to use nuclear weapons on a large scale, at least so far, demonstrates that humanity *does* have some capacity for making the right call when it comes to existential-level questions.

So what does a world post-post-World War II order look like? Well, we're already starting to see it emerge. Brexit—the departure of Great Britain from the European Union following the tumultuous plebiscite in June 2016—is more than a crack in the post-World War II order, it's more like a large sheet of rock crumbling off its face. If the EU continues to fracture, and the political and economic self-interests of European countries move away from each other, European politics may look more like the past than they have since 1945. That is somewhat ominous, especially if rifts develop between France and Germany. Franco-German competition was at the root of three major European wars between 1870 and 1945. The fact that Russia, under the czar-like rule of Vladimir Putin, is deliberately trying to sharpen tensions between EU countries doesn't help.

Who's a superpower in the 21st century world, and why, is also changing. The United States is seeing its superpower status, both economic and political, ebb away fairly rapidly. American political and military dominance in the world was badly and perhaps fatally injured by the failed intervention in Iraq from 2003 to 2011 and its open-ended and inconclusive involvement in Afghanistan since 2001. That's not to say that the U.S. has been or soon will be eclipsed as a military power by another country, but military power simply doesn't matter the way it used to anymore. If there is any doubt about that, one need only ask the last leader of the Soviet Union, Mikhail Gorbachev, who once commanded the world's second most powerful military, but found it useless in preventing the breakup of his country.

It seems beyond reasonable argument that China is now a superpower, though the Chinese tend to use their superpower status differently than the United States, Soviet Union and British Empire before her. I will discuss the role of China in the world, and how climate change is handing global leadership to the Chinese on a silver platter, in Chapter 8.3.

The role of Russia in the post-post-World War II order is something of a question mark. It seems pretty likely that Putin will remain in control of Russia so long as he remains alive. Unlike Stalin—to whom he is often compared—Putin has no broader ideological objective to serve, no revolution to defend, and apparently no serious interest in who holds power after he's gone. At least Putin realizes he can't take it with him. Whatever havoc Putin causes on the world stage in the time left to him we can't quite predict, but Russia will probably always be a prominent player, with one important caveat: her economy is overwhelmingly dependent on fossil fuels, and Putin doesn't give a damn about climate change. Where the Chinese are pragmatic enough to see the benefit in managing a transition from fossil fuels to renewables, it's harder to imagine a Putin-led Russia having any patience with a project like that. Climate change may hit Russia's world status harder than anyone else's.

An ominous subject that deserves at least a few words—but that I don't want to dwell on—is the possibility of a major global conflict in the future, "World War III," for lack of a better term. As a historian looking at the recent (~500 years) past, I can't rule it out. There have not really been two world wars. Depending on how you define "world war," one can argue that since the beginning of the 1600s there have been five: the Thirty Years' War, the Seven Years/French and Indian War, the French Revolutionary and Napoleonic Wars, World War I and World War II. At almost 75 years and counting since VE and VJ Day, we are, historically speaking, overdue for another one. The fact that climate change will put much greater stress on the world's resources raises the odds in favor of such a conflict. Even the Pentagon, whose commander-in-chief is currently a climate denier, understands this.

A world war is unquestionably a terrible calamity. When the world really goes off its rocker on a large scale, as it last did in the early 1940s, no one can predict where the chips will fall. But large-scale conflicts do have the potential to bring extremely rapid systemic change. That happened in both World War I and II. The thing about mega-wars is that they never end up being about whatever the trigger was that started them. (World War II was not principally about the Danzig Corridor in Poland, even though that's what precipitated it). Big wars have a way of settling much larger issues lurking behind them. If a major global conflict were to break out in the next few years or decades, I have little doubt that it would somehow involve the question *what are we going to do about climate change?* even if that question has nothing to do with what causes the shooting to start.

The end of the post-World War II order is the largest-scale shift in global politics and economics to occur in this century. In many ways it marks the end of society as most of us have known it. However, as I said in the introduction, that does *not* mean "the end of history." It just means the beginning of a new phase in history.

CHAPTER 7.2: ENDING: THE AGE OF FOSSIL FUELS

Although many of the issues surrounding climate change are very complex, the root of it is fairly simple. As a global society we've got to stop using fossil fuels. There are just no two ways about that. Much hand-wringing occurs when considering the follow-up questions, *"Can* we?" or *"Will* we?" I think the answers to these questions are almost self-evident. Yes, we can, and yes, we will. It's not like we have much of a choice.

Believe it or not, the end of fossil fuels has already begun, and their extinction is already significantly advanced. It's easy to scoff at that, given the ubiquitous nature of cars, petroleum, plastics and everything else we use fossil fuels for. Not long ago I gave a presentation on the history of climate change to a group of elementary school kids. By chance the school was located on the same block as a Phillips 76 gas station, visible through the window. Talking about the imminent end of fossil fuels while literally standing in the shadow of an oil company billboard can create some cognitive dissonance. But there are good reasons for predicting the end of the age of fossils.

Beyond the simple fact that the link between fossil fuel burning and harmful global warming is absolutely established, the biggest and most important sign that we're soon to exit the fossil fuel era is that the fossil companies themselves have no real plans for long-term survival. As I set out in Chapter 3, documents from Exxon's files prove that the company knew of its impending extinction no later than the 1970s, in memos that clearly show understanding that the world would have to draw down fossil fuel usage dramatically in the early part of this century. Given their immense political power, their unlimited financial resources and a 40-year head start, did the oil majors seek to develop a plan to transition out of their business model and reinvent themselves to survive in a fossil-free future? They did nothing of the kind. Instead, they invested money in lobbyists and denialist PR campaigns to try to prevent people from waking up to the truth.

Step back a moment and think about how damning that really is. We're talking about the largest, richest and most powerful corporations on Earth. They had money to burn and 40 years to build a lifeboat for themselves and their businesses, and *that* was the best idea they could come up with? *Really?* That's nothing short of pathetic.

This strategic failure shows us three important things about the fossil fuel industry. First, the fact that they could not bring themselves to face the problem of climate change honestly shows us that there is something about climate change so terrifying to fossil executives that they simply can't face it. Even sharing that truth with their shareholders—the people whose money they are responsible for—would have tanked the value of their companies and their industry. That means they fully understood that climate change is not merely a game-changer for them, but a game-*ender*.

Second, it shows us that the capacity for strategic thinking and conceptual innovation, on the level of fundamental business models, is surprisingly shallow for companies with such enormous resources. You'd think, with the financial ability to hire the brightest talent and the most forward-thinking entrepreneurs, that they'd have the best and the brightest in technology, marketing, finance and environmental science working for them—*if* their industry had any kind of future. But people like that don't work for oil companies. Instead they work for technology companies. The inability of an industry to attract talent from a younger generation is a telltale sign that it's on its last legs, because the talented young people who would otherwise be working there know it's a career dead-end. ExxonMobil does business essentially the same way its progenitor, Rockefeller's Standard Oil, did business when it began in 1870. Who wants to work for an industry that was cutting-edge when Ulysses S. Grant was in the White House?

Third, it demonstrates a remarkable lack of faith by the fossil fuel companies in the continued utility and dominance of their product. Trying to muddy the waters on climate change and appealing to lobbyists to help them out through manipulating the levers of government shows that the fossil companies understand their market dominance is supported by purely artificial means, such as government subsidies and tax breaks. Fossil companies *themselves* don't believe in their own products! They don't sell products that people want and are excited about. They know full well that their product—petroleum and other fossil fuels—is something that most people *don't* want, wish they didn't have to buy, and in most cases would abandon the first instant a viable alternative comes along. The fossil industry doesn't even believe in itself or the value of what it gives to the world. From a basic business perspective you can see what a terrible economic bargain fossil fuels are.

There is an interesting metric that suggests that oil may have already begun a terminal decline. In early 2019, Pew Charitable Trusts crunched a bunch of economic data to measure how and to what degree U.S. states have recovered their tax revenues since the Great Recession. Pew sampled data starting in early 2011—the depth of the recession—up until the last quarter of 2018. Many states have recovered extremely well: California's tax revenues are up 29.1% from the depth of the recession, Colorado's 34.5%, and New York's 18.2%. But some states' tax revenue has not recovered, and in many cases they've lost ground. Wyoming's tax collections in 2018 were 37.7% *less* than at the worst point of the recession. Oklahoma's declined 6% and Louisiana's 4.7%. Alaska's economy has cratered—their tax revenues were a whopping *83.7%* lower in 2018 than they were at the worst of the Great Recession.

What do all the states whose tax bases declined have in common? Their economies are based primarily on fossil fuel extraction. Even the state which was far and away the leader in growing its tax revenues, North Dakota, portends the end of oil. North Dakota's tax base spiked by a surreal 58.7% during the recovery. That's because fracking—the high-risk, high-pollution squeezing of the last pitiful drops of oil and gas out of rock layers previously deemed useless—has artificially inflated North Dakota's economy. Fracking (hydraulic fracturing) is a last-ditch, economically desperate form of fossil fuel extraction. Fracking is the fossil fuel industry equivalent of an alcoholic who's run out of booze frantically ransacking his house in the hopes that there's still a bottle stashed somewhere that he might have forgotten about. Nobody would even take the idea of fracking seriously unless the economics of traditional oil are irrevocably broken.

To hear fossil fuel companies themselves talk publicly about climate change and renewable energy, of course you hear a lot of self-justification and reassurance. Yes, they say, we understand climate change exists, and we *do* care (really?), but fossils will be a significant part of the world's energy mix for decades to come, so they say. I'm not so sure. I believe that climate change and its effects are accelerating. Everything is moving faster. Given the accelerating effects of climate change and the sudden recent surge in public demand, all around the world, to do something about it, I believe the collapse of the fossil fuel industry will be swift and virtually total.

There is historical precedent for such a change. In the early 19th century, the economies of the world's two largest colonial empires, the British and French empires, were built largely on slavery. The production of sugar cane from the West Indies was especially profitable, and France's colony of St. Domingue—now Haiti—was once the richest colonial possession on planet Earth. Although decades of abolitionist sentiment preceded it, slavery was abolished fairly abruptly, by the British in 1833 and the French in 1848 (following a previous abolition in 1794, during the revolutionary period, that didn't stick). Other important economies, such as Spain, also abolished slavery in roughly the same period. The one laggard was the United States, where slavery hung on until 1865, but even that was barely more than three decades since Britain's abolition. After centuries of economic dominance, slavery collapsed relatively quickly. It still exists (unfortunately) in various corners of the world, but nowhere is it legally protected, much less the central basis of major global economies.

The phaseout of fossil fuels may follow a similar pattern. A long period of warning, agitation and public unease with fossil fuels and their effects over the past few decades, principally driven by growing understanding of climate change, resembles the slow burn of anti-slavery sentiment in many countries in the 18th and early 19th century. Then this sentiment flares into sudden bursts of activism, usually spearheaded by charismatic individuals; in the abolitionist narrative, think of William Wilberforce in Britain and William Lloyd Garrison in the United States. (Today's equivalent in the climate change space may be teenage activist Greta Thunberg). Finally, activism results in a sudden rapid shift resulting in a rash of governmental activity abolishing and outlawing the problematic institution. Just as it would have been a bad financial move to go into the business of trading slaves to the British West Indies in 1830, it's today a bad financial move to go into the fossil fuel business in 2020. You don't need to be clairvoyant to see this coming.

What would a world without fossil fuel dependence be like? I'm a historian, not a futurist, so I'm less sanguine on making specific projections, but I'm willing to make a few guesses. Patterns of life and work based around the automobile will probably change. Just as the development of cars expanded suburbs, a lesser reliance on cars will possibly cause suburbs to retract, cities to become denser and more people to work at home, or closer to home. Certain things based around instinctive use of cars will become rarer: drive-in fast food joints, for instance. (This is already happening; how many drive-in theaters are there anymore?) Trucking goods from place to place may decline in favor of heavier reliance on rail transport, which can be powered by renewable energy. We'll probably eat a lot more food produced locally and take fewer plane trips. We'll own less and rent, borrow and share more. This too is already underway—services like ZipCar, Uber and Airbnb are the vanguard of it.

This won't necessarily be bad. If car dominance declines, think of all the space that will suddenly become available particularly in dense urban cores—all the parking lots, highway ramps and car dealerships that could be turned into affordable housing, or parks studded with solar panels and small windmills, or planted with trees to sequester carbon from the atmosphere. Housing developments and apartment complexes could be built to incorporate small-scale and community gardens where food could be locally raised. People would know their neighbors again. Wherever a strong sense of community takes hold, people usually flourish.

CHAPTER 7.3: ENDING: THE AGE OF IDEOLOGIES

It may seem at first blush strange to project this as a consequence of climate change, but the era of our history defined principally by the struggle of ideologies and ideologically-organized ways of life may be a thing of the past in a warmed world. This is related to the previous endings I've discussed, but warrants a section of its own.

Ideologies of one kind or another have existed throughout human history, and struggles between ideological belief systems have often been an engine of historical change. In early modern Europe, for instance, the conflict between Catholicism and Protestant Christianity, which raged from the early 16th to the late 17th centuries, was highly significant. But it was really the French Revolution, which began in 1789, that brought ideological competition to the forefront. The development of nationalism in the 19th century was related to the sharpening of ideologies. The fusion of ideology with ideas of economic organization—Marxism, developed in the 1840s, is a paradigm example—raised the stakes and made ideology even more important. Although I contend that World War II was more about resources than about ideology, there clearly *was* an ideological component to it, and certainly the U.S.-Soviet standoff of the Cold War was ideologically-based.

Climate change, however, presents a challenge to ideology. There's a reason why you find most climate change denial on the right-leaning side of the political spectrum: to combat climate change effectively, some form of large-scale government involvement in the economy is inescapable. This is understandably threatening to ideological belief systems that maintain, as an axiom, that government involvement in the economy (regulation) is always bad and unnecessary. When facts conflict with belief systems, people are usually more motivated to deny the facts than they are to reexamine belief systems. This is a trait of human nature.

Noting how climate change is especially unwelcome to believers in one particular ideology, however, does not mean that climate change validates any *other* ideology. Climate change doesn't care about your politics; it doesn't care about anything. A Marxist clutching a hefty tome of *Das Kapital* is no better equipped to deal with climate change than a free-market Libertarian waving around a copy of *Atlas Shrugged*. The point is that climate change is a problem that ideology isn't really much help in solving. As global warming pinches increasingly harder, the vast effort that people have generally been putting into fighting ideological battles over the last 250 years will have to be redirected to pursuits more closely aligned with the problem at hand.

This isn't to say that particular people, institutions or nations won't *try* to use ideological solutions to deal with climate change. Surely they will. Particularly if climate change generates conflict between groups or nations—and it probably will—ideologies will undoubtedly become intertwined with the various issues in these conflicts. So I'm not saying that ideology will go away. But I think it's more likely that the necessity of dealing with climate change will be the dog that wags the tail of ideology, not the other way around.

Given the tumultuous nature of history for the past two and a half centuries, the prospect of living in a world where practical and environmental considerations eclipse battles over ideology is perhaps an attractive one. A relaxation of partisanship would be a welcome state of affairs in the United States, where political battles over everything have proved increasingly exhausting over the past 50 years. Climate change, rising to the level of an existential threat, holds out the prospect of bringing at least some temporary unity to the battlegrounds between political parties in various countries.

Climate change may bring people and communities together in unexpected ways. Unity and cooperation are common responses to large-scale disaster—and we'll have more than our share of disasters in the era of climate change. In November 1980, a fire at the MGM Grand Hotel in Las Vegas killed 85 people and caused the rapid evacuation of thousands more. After the disaster, sociologists studied the behavior of people involved, and found that comparatively few people panicked and actions reflecting desperation and selfishness were relatively rare. I recall well-publicized instances of altruism and cooperation in climate-related disasters, such as a Mexican restaurant giving away free tacos in the wake of Hurricane Sandy in 2012, or a Lowe's customer buying an expensive power generator for a complete stranger in the run-up to Hurricane Irma in 2017. Ideological differences seem like abstract luxuries when winds lash and seas rise.

A large-scale, across-the-board worldwide effort to battle climate change—which is the response we really need—would probably have very significant positive effects on partisanship and ideological strife. Nations that were formerly competitors will be forced to work together toward common goals and common welfare. Climate change will affect the Israelis and the Palestinians alike, and they live in such proximity to one another that cooperation to deal with the effects of climate change in the Holy Land is mandatory. It's difficult to see how effective efforts to deal with droughts, water scarcity and sea level rise on the Korean peninsula are supposed to happen without close cooperation between the governments of North and South Korea. The indifference of climate change to beliefs or ideologies definitely has an upside.

Indeed, there's much more I could say about the possibilities for cooperation and the potential effect this collective effort might have on humanity as a whole. I'll leave that discussion to Chapter 8.4. Suffice it to say for now, our history being dominated, as it has been for much of the past 250 years, by struggles between ideologies—revolutions to incite (or defend), socioeconomic systems to validate, utopias to build (or prevent)—seems unlikely in the face of the awesome challenges of climate change. Making our world livable is going to take most of our energy for the foreseeable future.

CHAPTER 7.4: ENDING: BUSINESS AS USUAL

The original IPCC Report of 1990, and many other climate change analyses, projected a climate change scenario they called "Business as Usual" (BAU). Essentially this was a worst-case scenario, where humanity continues to burn fossil fuels at an increased rate and there's little effort to reduce CO_2 emissions. Life in a BAU world would be pretty frightening—but honestly I don't think we're going to get there. BAU is ending. It's too costly to continue, economically.

This is really, as far as climate change is concerned, the meat in the coconut. The way we do business, the way our economy works, and the way we measure wealth is going to change—and that's exactly why climate change terrifies many people, because instinctively they know this is true. An economy based on consumer goods, consumer spending and the manufacture and sale of stuff, treating natural resources and the ecology of the planet as unlimited resources that will always be there and always exploitable, is simply no longer possible.

In early 2019, a group of Finnish scientists from the BIOS Research Unit issued a report to the United Nations which will be a significant part of the U.N. Global Sustainable Development Report, due out later in the year. The report is blunt in its ultimate conclusion: capitalism as we've known it for the past few centuries it is finished. And like many other effects of climate change, the metamorphosis of capitalism is already underway.

The key metric in the 2019 BIOS report is what's called EROEI, Energy Return on Energy Invested. It's a measurement of how much energy you have to put in to get out a certain amount of energy. For example, petroleum doesn't burn itself. You have to light it with something. A pilot light is energy invested; whatever you get out of the fuel you light is the energy return. The BIOS scientists observed that, even now, economic actors are beginning to employ more and more fuels—mainly renewables—that have lower EROEI than fossil fuels. And fossil fuels *themselves* are declining in EROEI. That's because the fossils that are left, such as tar sands, are harder to get to than the low-hanging-fruit reserves that have been harvested up until now. The world economic system is built on very high EROEI fuels. Now that those numbers are declining, the world economy is, as a result, changing.

Until relatively recently, EROEI has been viewed as a stumbling block to transitioning the world's economy to renewable fuels. Those people who are pessimists that such a transition is even possible would often cite EROEI as "proof"—that because fossils have such a high EROEI, the immutable laws of economics dictate that businesses and companies would never under any circumstances choose energy sources with lower EROEI values. Supposedly this means that we will *always* opt to use fossil fuels so long as they exist, and solar, wind and other renewables can never compete with them in any serious way.

In my view, EROEI-based pessimism is more of a belief system than an economic or historical reality. In the 1990s and particularly the decade of the 2000s, a theory called "peak oil" had a brief surge of popularity in small circles of economists and academics, particularly on the Internet. "Peak oil," based entirely on somewhat spurious theories about economics, holds that the world will enter an economic crisis just after the supply of fossil fuels reaches its highest level (peaks), and as demand continues to rise. Peak oilers' favorite pastime was to argue about when the peak would occur, or if it had already occurred. Curiously, most peak oilers weren't that interested in climate change. They weren't deniers in the classic sense, but most were far more concerned with the economic wreckage they predicted as a result of running low on oil as opposed to the effects of climate change. The more pessimistic peak oilers would trot out EROEI figures of fossil fuels versus renewables to support a defeatist argument that transitioning to renewables was economically impossible—thus locking in the doomsday predictions of what happens when we run low on oil. Peak oil as a belief system reached its zenith just before the Great Recession of 2008. It's relatively hard to find peak oilers around today. Most of the prominent peak oil blogs and forums have been shut down or abandoned.

The point I'm trying to make is that the central assumption on which peak oil—and other arguments about the impossibility of transition to renewable energy—is based has already been proven false. Fuels with higher EROEIs are not automatically a better bargain than sources of power with lower EROEI numbers, and we will not always make economic decisions about what fuels to use based on those numbers. Furthermore, if the EROEI on fossils themselves are declining, that means that the low-cost fuels we're used to are rapidly becoming a thing of the past—which means that we might as well choose the fuels that *don't* contribute to global warming, since the EROEIs we supposedly want are no longer available anyway. Essentially, EROEI is becoming less important than it used to be.

Economies as we now know them are based on cheap (high-EROEI) fuels. The dominance of the automobile, beginning in the early 1900s but especially taking off in the 1920s, was built entirely around fuel being abundant and affordable. "A car in every garage and a chicken in every pot," which was Herbert Hoover's campaign slogan when he ran for President in 1928, assumed fuels were cheap and affordable. The business model for

McDonald's hamburgers—you place your order, drive up, are handed your food through the window, and you drive away—assumed fuels were cheap and affordable. So did the business model of the beef supplier, who got its cows driven to the plant in trucks or hauled by die-sel-powered locomotives, and the manufacturer of the cheap plastic trinkets in the Happy Meal you were just handed, who made those trinkets from cheap petrole-um. This is all going to change as a result of climate change.

What it does *not* mean is collapse, famine, poverty and apocalypse. There is not one way to structure an economy or provide for the material needs of people in a society. People develop alternatives and work-arounds; they already have. Ten or fifteen years ago, if you lived in Seattle and had a business meeting in Cincinnati, you had to drive to the airport, get on a plane, check into a hotel, go to your meeting and do your business, and then fly back home. Today you can attend that meeting via Zoom or some other software, and save your compa-ny thousands of dollars it would otherwise have spent to send you to Cincinnati. If your company, for whatever reason, tomorrow decided "We will never again pay to send anyone to a business conference," it probably wouldn't even be that big a deal.

Though it's hard to imagine when talking to an econ-omist, economic models *do* change. They have to. Just as the world does business differently than it did when modern capitalism began to develop in the Italian city-states of the Renaissance, so will it do business different-ly—*radically* differently, I think—twenty or even ten years from now. Climate change is imposing a new set of constraints on what is possible in the economic sphere. Some things that are possible now, and that we take for granted, will become impossible, prohibitively expensive, or so obviously unwise as to be off-limits as viable options. Other things that are *not* possible now, and that we can't imagine could ever be practical or even desirable, will become not only possible and desirable, but routine and taken for granted to the point where we won't even notice them until someone points them out. This is how history works.

Business as usual is dead. Stick a fork in it: it's done. Whatever our future economy is going to look like is impossible to predict now, but there's no going back to the old one.

CHAPTER 7.5: ENDING: "GROWTH"

This subject is closely related to the one in the last sub-chapter. BAU, as we've known it up until now, is built on an overarching concept enshrined as the single measurement of economic success: "growth." If BAU and the era of cheap fuels on which it is based is ending, it stands to reason that "growth," whatever it really means, is ending too. This is what scares a lot of people, because they can't imagine an economy, or a lifestyle, without "growth." The reality is that it's much easier, and much less scary, to imagine such an economy than you might think at first.

You may have noticed I put the word "growth" in air-quotes, because it's a word whose meaning is uncertain. "Growth" in an economic sense is one of those words where everybody thinks they know what it means, but when you drill down into it, it becomes harder to pin down. You could make a statement like, "The GDP of the United States grew by 3.5% last year," or "My company's earnings grew by 7%." But what those numbers really mean depend entirely on what you count, and how you measure "growth."

In August 2018, British billionaire Jeremy Grantham, who has studied the phenomenon of economic bubbles, issued a paper that contained a somewhat startling con-clusion: despite what most of us think, the world econ-omy hasn't really "grown" at all in decades. In fact, it's shrinking. Grantham gets there by figuring in the cost of replacement of extractive industries, soil depletion and other externalities—in other words, the cost of fixing the damage to the environment that economic activities cost. If you figure in those costs, which are rising sharp-ly, the profits of the world economy in the past few years are dwarfed by them—meaning that our econo-mies, at least in the West, are shrinking, not growing. But of course, the way accountants and investors meas-ure economic performance, those externalities are usu-ally ignored. A copper mining company doesn't figure into its balance sheet the cost of replacing the copper it's taken out of the ground for decades, or ameliorating the environmental damage the extraction causes. They count only the cost it takes to mine the copper and ship it to market. If the company's financials took externalities into account, it wouldn't look like a profitable company at all. In fact, it'd be bankrupt.

A variation of this same phenomenon—externalities eventually hitting the balance sheet, despite everyone's best efforts—is one of the reasons why fossil companies know they're doomed. In their business it's called the "stranded assets problem." When an oil company discovers a new oil field, even before they sink a single drill bit into the ground, they're allowed, by their accountants and the law, to count the future value of that entire oil field as a *present* asset on their balance sheets. If something comes along in the future (like, I don't know, maybe *climate change?*) that makes it impossible for them to drill that field, suddenly they lose it as an asset, and the value of their company goes down. Stranded assets are a problem that, again despite their enormous wealth and political protection, fossil companies haven't been able to figure out how to solve. They know they're sitting on a $24 trillion time bomb, and they haven't a clue how to defuse it. When the bomb explodes, their industry dies. This is why climate change terrifies the fossil companies so much.

The idea that Western economies aren't really growing, but actually shrinking, is entirely consistent with historical observation. The economy of the United States began to contract in the 1970s, when the long post-World War II manufacturing boom ended and most heavy manufacturing moved overseas. That's when the steel mills of western Pennsylvania went dark and turned into the ruins that gave the region its nickname as the "Rust Belt." It's no coincidence that President Richard Nixon took the U.S. off the gold standard about that same time, that the economy was rocked by two recessions (in 1973 and 1979) heavily related to energy costs, and that the American auto industry lost its dominance and market share to cars manufactured principally in Asia. The American economy shrank, pure and simple. The economic activities that Americans have engaged in since the 1970s are primarily related to the delivery of services, technology and financial speculation, all of which are much more susceptible to artificial manipulation of value than the hard goods American companies were manufacturing in the decades after the war. If you doubt that, look at what caused the stock market crashes of 1987, 2000 and 2008. Example: in early 2000, Pets.com was one of the hottest companies in America, raising $82 million in its first IPO. When the company liquidated only a few months later, its stock was worth 19 cents a share. Somebody—a *lot* of somebodies—obviously made a terrible mistake about what Pets.com was really worth.

The loss of value of the U.S. economy, in real terms, comports with our lived experience too. Wages are declining. If the economy was really "growing," shouldn't median wages and purchasing power be going up, not down? Home ownership, once the *sina qua non* of economic success in America, has generally declined even from levels seen during the Great Recession. Younger people can't buy houses anymore because they're drowning in student debt, their jobs pay too little, and the cost of health insurance is too high. There are towns in many parts of the United States, such as in eastern Kentucky, where unemployment has been in double digits for nearly 30 years. This isn't the fault of a particular politician, political party or even an ideology. Voting for someone who promises to "put America back to work again"—a slogan used by Ronald Reagan in 1980, Bill Clinton in 1992 and Mitt Romney in 2012—isn't going to make any difference. The economy has changed. "Growth" is an illusion.

At least in the United States, observing the coming generational and demographic shifts, which I'll talk more about in the next subchapter, should put the final nail in the coffin of the idea of "growth." At the present time, for the first time in American history, significantly greater numbers of people—principally Baby Boomers—are exiting the workforce, through retirement and death, than the number of people, age 15 to 19, who are about to enter it. Soon the U.S. economy will have vastly more retirees trying to live off pensions, 401Ks and savings than the number of active workers earning money in the economy. Even using economists' and accountants' spurious measurements that ignore the cost of externalities, "growth" is impossible under these conditions. No one knows what to do about it.

So again, we see in the case of a climate-changed world that what's going to be our future is already beginning in our present, and can be observed in the recent past. Our economy isn't really "growing" at all. Given that we've already been living without "growth" since *The Brady Bunch* was still on the air, the notion that a future economy will also not deliver "growth" really shouldn't be that scary.

The good news is that, because "growth" that investors respond to is largely in the eye of the beholder, we can—and will—simply redefine what we mean by "growth," if we don't replace it entirely with a new and more realistic measurement. What if we pegged a company's stock value not to how much more money it (supposedly) made over the past quarter, but how much more efficient it was at managing its resources than it was the previous quarter? What if we replaced *growth* with *sustainability*, in terms of measuring economic success? And by *sustainability* I mean fundamental sustainability, not just recycle bins and electric cars. If every ton of CO_2 a company doesn't produce—or, better yet, actually sequesters by planting trees or other carbon sinks—results in an uptick of its value, suddenly "growth" takes on a whole new dimension. An investor can still get a 7% return on paper, but what we count as "return" can be anything we decide it is.

In a climate-changed future, our businesses and our homes will have to use less energy and generate less waste. That's the absolute, immutable truth about the future of climate change. That truth becomes a threat to our way of life only so long as we define our way of life as being tied to using energy and generating waste with impunity. In this sense, the most valuable work that we can do to adapt to global warming is not to build seawalls or windmills, though that will have to be done too. The truly valuable work in climate change adaptation will be in our heads and our hearts. We have it in our power to redefine, any time we want, the value of our lives. If you take only one message from this book, let it be this one.

CHAPTER 7.6: ENDING: OWNERSHIP OF THE WORLD BY AN OLDER GENERATION

I keep returning to the subject of World War II as being so crucial to climate change, and here's how it is in yet another way. When the G.I.s returned to American shores after giving Hitler and Tojo what-for, one of the things they did, in addition to going to college, getting jobs and buying houses, was that they had a lot of sex. The Baby Boom generation, now usually defined as births between 1946 and 1964, has dominated the American political, economic and social landscape for most of the time since at least the 1960s. The Baby Boom also happened in many other countries too. But the ownership of the world by Baby Boomers is, quite rapidly, coming to an end. This should be among the least controversial arguments I make in this book: it's simple mathematics.

Talking about generational shifts is a bit of a tricky business. There are undoubtedly Baby Boomers who are reading this book, and there are also Millennials and post-Millennials who are reading it too. At first blush it may look, in the discussion that follows, as if I'm talking about both generations without acknowledging that I'm also talking *to* them. What I'm trying to do here is maintain some sense of historical objectivity. It's also impossible to talk about generations and generational identity without committing one of the cardinal sins of historiography: generalizing. I'm fully aware that no generation can be painted all with one brush. That said, I still think the exercise is valuable; just bear with me.

The oldest of the Baby Boomers are now, in 2019, in their early 70s—well past traditional retirement age. The youngest of them are only ten years away. This generation's prime productive years, in terms of work, economic output, cultural expression and family-building, were roughly from the late 1970s to the 2000s. Except for the handful of hardy survivors born in 1964 who will live to be 110 or more, every single Baby Boomer in America has fewer days ahead of them than they do behind them. Boomers, your generation is losing its grip on the levers of power, economic influence and cultural dominance. When the world does finally slip out of your hands, the resulting shift will be massive. I already discussed in the last subchapter the demographic fact that the generations already in, and about to enter, the workforce are significantly smaller than the generation exiting it, which means the economy is going to have to be fundamentally reorganized to function on an entirely different model, just for that reason alone.

If you'll indulge me for a bit of wonky historical number-crunching, I'd like to show you how generational shifts have worked in American history by utilizing an easy shorthand: grouping U.S. Presidents by generation, and seeing both how long particular generations managed to hang around the White House, as well as how old their members were when they got into office. A generation's representation in the Presidency is a rough way of estimating who generally held political and economic power in the United States in various eras. This *does* relate to climate change, I assure you; I'll connect the dots for you at the end.

The ages of presidents at inauguration, with only a few exceptions, tend to skew older toward the end of a generation's turn in power. The first generation of Americans, those who were born before the Declaration of Independence and most of whom had participated in the Revolution, was remarkably reluctant to turn over power to a new generation. It took nine presidents before a permanent generational change occurred, and the last two members of this generation, Andrew Jackson (born 1767) and William Henry Harrison (born 1773), were the oldest to hold the office, at 61 and 68, respectively. The Civil War was a formative experience for the generation who lived through it, and seven men who'd either worn a uniform in the Civil War or paid someone else to wear one in their place held the presidency between 1869 and 1901. The oldest of them at inauguration—Harrison in 1889 and Cleveland at his second swearing-in in 1893—falling toward the end of this list, both 55. (The last Civil War veteran elected, William McKinley, was 54).

The picture gets more interesting in the 20th century. Excluding Eisenhower who had a military career and is something of an outlier, five veterans of World War II—

John F. Kennedy, Lyndon Johnson, Richard Nixon, Gerald Ford and the first George Bush—sat in the Oval Office, the youngest at inauguration being Kennedy (43) and the oldest Bush (64). If you define "the World War II generation" as people born in the 20th century who were old enough to serve in the military during the conflict, even if they actually did not, the list should also include Ronald Reagan, who sat out the war making movies in Hollywood, and Jimmy Carter, who entered the U.S. Naval Academy in 1943 but did not graduate until after the war was over.

When the first Bush was defeated for reelection in 1992, power passed to the Baby Boom generation. Bill Clinton was the youngest Baby Boomer president at 46. The second Bush was born in the same year he was, 1946, but he came to power eight years later; Obama, the sole representative of the late Baby Boom (born 1961), was 47 when he took the oath. Donald Trump, the oldest president ever elected, was 70, and shares his birth year with Clinton and the second Bush. Even if Trump's opponent had won in 2016 the trend wouldn't have been broken; Hillary Clinton was 69 at the time of the election.

What's even more fascinating is that the presidency seems to skip generations, or almost skip them. No one born in the thirteen years between 1809 (Abraham Lincoln) and 1822 (Ulysses Grant) was ever elected president. Only one U.S. President, Eisenhower, came from the entire generation of Americans born in the nearly quarter-century between 1884 (Truman) and 1908 (LBJ). Another entire generation was skipped between the first

George Bush's birth in 1924 and the birth year of three of the four most recent presidents, 1946. Political power in the United States does not draw equally from generations.

Of course, today in 2019, it's the Millennial generation that's rapidly coming up—and, perhaps welcome news for you Millennials, the transition to your ownership and control, I think, will be much faster than previous generational shifts. And here's where this story is relevant to climate change: the reason for a quick transition from Boomers to Millennials is that action on climate change is time-sensitive. It must be done *now*, and the Millennials and their successors deeply feel this urgency. They also feel that previous generations have failed them. It's difficult to argue that they're wrong. Particularly in the first half of 2019, which saw widespread climate marches and school strikes and the activism of people like Greta Thunberg and the *Juliana v. U.S.* plaintiffs, the message from the younger generations has been made very clear: "You (older generations) had your chance. You failed and there's no time left to try again, so step aside and let us take the helm."

For this reason—the urgency Millennials and post-Millennials feel about climate change—I think it likely that you Millennials will permanently seize political and economic power quite soon, and that this power will pass directly from the Baby Boomers to the Millennials while entirely or mostly skipping the generation in between, "Generation X." (That's my generation; I was born in the early 1970s). Protestations by older generations to the effect of, "We *are* working on it, so trust us," or "You aren't yet ready to handle this," which is what politicians repeatedly say when cornered by young people on climate change issues, aren't going to mollify anyone. The Millennials won't take no for an answer. They will not bargain for power, and on issues involving climate change they will not compromise. Try negotiating with Greta Thunberg on gradual solutions to climate change. It would be like trying to make a deal with William Lloyd Garrison or Frederick Douglass on gradual abolition of slavery: you just couldn't do it.

The Millennials are a generation whose identity will be defined by climate change. What is ending, therefore, is ownership of the world by a generation whose identity is defined by something else—*anything* else. That is welcome news to some, but others will undoubtedly take it hard. For better or for worse, though, this is how history works.

CHAPTER 8: WHAT IS BEGINNING?

So much talk about climate change is apocalyptic, and framed in terms of endings. But as one era of history ends, another begins. The thesis of this book, remember, is that climate change is not "the end of history." It's always more difficult to predict the future than to analyze the past, so taking stock of what's beginning with climate change is a harder call. But here too I think we

can make some educated guesses by projecting historical analysis forward.

CHAPTER 8.1: BEGINNING: THE WORLD OF THE MILLENNIALS

I spent the last part of Chapter 7 talking about how ownership of the world and political power appears like-ly to pass out of the hands of the Baby Boom generation relatively quickly, and become assumed by Millennials, without passing through Generation X. Let's now spend some thought on what the world of the Millennials might look like.

For openers, you Millennials' ownership and control of the world is likely to last a very long time. You will be quite young when you inherit it, and you'll try to hold onto it until every last one of you is dead because you won't trust anyone else to run the world. Let's revisit again what we learned in the thought experiment in-volving the birthdates and generational identities of American presidents. The generation of the American Revolution held power for 50 years, and both the Civil War and World War II generations for 32 years each. The Baby Boom generation has been in power in the United States for 27 years, since 1992. For reasons I talked about in the last subchapter, you know why I think their time in the saddle is almost up.

Imagine a Millennial president—a John F. Kennedy for a new generation—determined to tackle climate change, heralding not merely a generational but a cultural shift upon taking power. The beginning of the Millennial generation is usually defined as 1982, so a Millennial born at that time could be elected president now. Someone born in 1982 would be 38 in 2020 and 42 in 2024. Theodore Roosevelt, the youngest-ever person to *serve* as president, came into the White House at age 42 upon the assassination of William McKinley; John F. Kennedy, the youngest-ever person *elected* president, was 43.

Now imagine someone born late in the Millennial generation, say in the year 2000. As we've seen, the average age of a president tends to skew upward toward the end of a generation's cycle in power. If a man or woman born in 2000 is as old as Donald Trump was when he was elected, this hypothetical late-Millennial could be in office in the year 2070. Those of us who were born before the Millennials came along will probably live out the remainder of our natural lives while they hold power.

Politically, the Millennial generation will be utterly consumed with the fight against climate change. Adaptation to climate change, and dealing with conflicts caused by or related to climate change, will be their dominant life experiences. Millennials, you will probably suffer from "climate change fatigue" and grow very tired of dealing with it. And the work won't be finished when your generation exits the stage of history, which means you'll have to teach your children how to adapt to climate change too.

Economically, the world the Millennials will build will operate on an entirely different set of values than our current economy does. Let me give you an example. If there's one thing that Millennials hate more than climate change, it's debt. The Baby Boom generation tended to see debt as a good and useful thing: cheap mortgages made it easy to buy property, and credit cards financed lavish lifestyles. Millennials have totally the opposite experience with debt. They see it as akin to slavery. I would regard it as highly likely that a Congress dominated by Millennials will eagerly and repeatedly pass debt relief and amnesty legislation, and a Millennial president would happily sign such legislation to ensure re-election. Student loans will probably be first to go, then credit cards, then mortgages. Absolution from student loan debt may not even have to wait until Millennials are in control. Older politicians seeking Millennials' votes are already figuring out this is a sure winner. Being a moneylender in the middle decades of the 21st century will be as bad a business to be in as fossil fuels.

The Millennial world will be innovative and adaptable, put together with odds and ends for functional purposes, some old, some new. It will be as much low-tech as high-tech. Due to the fact that the Millennial generation was raised from birth with personal technology and the ease with which they use it, we've developed a cultural assumption that Millennials are somehow "*the* technology generation," and that their relationship to technology is a part of their identity. I'm not convinced that's true, at least no more true than it is of any other generation. A climate-changed world will, as we know, have to move slower, use less energy and generate less waste, so Millennials are the prime candidates for a generation that may actually *disengage* from personal technology to a significant degree. As the values and desires that undergird the economy change in response to global warming, the supposedly "innate" lust to use a lot of technology may prove to be not so innate after all.

The idea of an economy and political system based on the collective values of the Millennial generation is no doubt a horrifying one to their elders, particularly the Baby Boom generation. But that's just how generational change works. After a while, the world just isn't yours anymore, and at some point you have to put up and shut up. Parents of the 1920s feared their kids were growing up to be hedonistic libertines; in the 1950s it was thought the next generation would be shiftless beatnik layabouts; in the 1960s the Baby Boomers were denounced as long-haired, drug-addled anarchists; today Millennials are mocked as "special snowflakes" with zero attention spans and endless lists of petty demands. You Millennials will be similarly aghast at the attitudes and behavior of your kids. To quote the movie *Star Trek VI* again, as the elderly Klingon ruler says to an aging Captain Kirk, "If there is to be a brave new world, our generation is going to have the hardest time living in it."

Speaking only for myself, I feel a great deal of optimism about the Millennials' world, which will be my world too—and yours. Despite the challenges and disasters that climate change presents us, there's every reason to believe that the world this energetic generation will build will be cleaner, fairer and more fulfilling a place to live than the world we live in now. It will undoubtedly be a hotter and perhaps more dangerous world, but there will be positive trade-offs as well.

CHAPTER 8.2: BEGINNING: A COOPERATIVE ECONOMY

As bad as it is, climate change will do one very good thing for us: it will force us to work together to overcome it. I've already alluded to this with a few examples, such as the need for Israelis and Palestinians to work together, and for North and South Korea to cooperate. I've also talked about how the values on which our economy is based must, and will, change. As the economy reinvents itself and the BAU model fades into the past, I think it likely that economic models based on cooperation will replace those rooted in competition.

Don't get me wrong here: I'm not talking about Communism or any other sort of political ideology. And competition for resources is likely to rise sharply in a warming world. But in order to move slower, use less energy and generate less waste while still delivering the necessities of life, economic actors will find it to their advantage to find ways to cooperate and to leverage each other's strengths. There will still be economic competition, but in many ways it may get "friendlier" than it is now.

Let's take a simple example, one well within the realm of today's possibilities. Imagine a restaurant out in the country somewhere that operates on a farm-to-table model. Just about everything the restaurant serves comes from within a five-mile radius. Fresh vegetables, grown on-site or in local community gardens, are always on the menu. Suppose the restaurant happens to be next to a pig farm. The pig farmer, who raises his livestock on-site, sells fresh pork to the restaurant at a discount. In turn, the restaurant delivers food cuttings and table scraps back to the farmer to feed his pigs. The restaurant might also make sausage that's sold at a local market, and the pig farmer might deliver buckets of pig manure to fertilize the restaurant's and the community's gardens. As symbiotic relationships develop between the restaurant, the pig farm, the market and the community gardens, more and more waste ends up getting put back into somebody else's operation, fewer miles are driven to deliver product or supplies, less energy is used and carbon emissions go down. And we've got a restaurant that serves tasty food, pigs raised in a healthy and humane environment, a garden popping with fresh vegetables and a market with great stuff to sell. The cooperative model here serves everyone well.

Now imagine something like this being done on a large scale with major corporations. Suppose somebody figured out a way to make a strong, sturdy material, suitable for making automobiles, from wood chips or some other biodegradable materials. A recycling plant could provide a steady supply of raw materials, from packaging and trash thrown away, that could be ground up and "cooked" into panels that could be used to make cars, which, when they reach the end of their useful life, are recycled and crushed back into raw materials for another go-round. The automobile manufacturer and the recycling plant might choose to locate their major facilities next door to each other. If they generate power locally, with solar panels or wind turbines, they could share the power, and if they generate more power than they need they could sell it to local communities—where most of their employees live—at a discount. Imagine if the automaker was the biggest in the country and the recycling plant handled wood chip waste from all over the world, delivered by sailing ship to the recycler's own docks. Almost every waste product from these two businesses could be recycled into raw materials for another business. *That's* a cooperative economic model.

There are numerous opportunities for this sort of cooperation. If companies begin to change their business models to value efficiency and conservation of resources over "growth," as we've already discussed, the incentives and rewards for finding angles for cooperative leveraging will multiply fast, because each one found will increase the measure of a company's success. Cooperation on this level will also become easier as interconnectedness rises as a cultural and societal value (see Subchapter 8.4). Add to this the carrot and stick of government—tax incentives for cooperation and regulations against wastefulness and carbon generation—and the entire economy could be tilted heavily in favor of cooperativeness.

I've mentioned a couple of times so far that climate change will result in an alteration of the basic values undergirding our economy. That's also true of our understanding of government's relationship to the economy. Many of the ideological battlegrounds of the 20th century focused on the degree to which government should intervene in economic affairs, and, especially in the last few decades, the side that believes that government should interfere as little as possible seems to have emerged victorious. It seems almost inevitable that the pendulum will swing in the opposite direction throughout most of this century, as the ideology that regards any government intervention as an anathema fades from prominence.

Government intervention will undoubtedly be required to address climate change, but in the coming years I think fewer and fewer people will be troubled by that. This is, after all, what happened in the Great Depression of the 1930s, when laissez-faire principles proved unrealistic to cope with the scale of the economic disaster. That's not to say the New Deal wasn't highly controversial—it was—but ultimately many of its central tenets, such as Social Security and unemployment insurance, were eventually written into the American social compact, however imperfectly. Protection against the dangers of climate change will, I believe, similarly be written into the social compact in this century. Government will play a key role in executing that compact.

A more cooperative economy may lead to some significant fringe benefits. The sharpness of economic cycles, boom and bust, could flatten out in a more cooperative system, or at least people, companies and industries will have more to lean on in hard times. A cooperative economy might even be recession-proof, especially if its nodes are dispersed to a lot of local businesses rather than most economic activity being centered in the hands of a few very large companies.

The economics of renewable power generation look especially good for creating durable jobs on a local level. Jobs in the solar industry can't be outsourced. Wherever solar farms are, you need to have people building, tending and repairing them, and because it's much cheaper and more efficient to use renewable energy close to where it's generated instead of transmitting it from distant plants, that means they'll be fairly close to the communities and businesses they serve. This is good news for those towns in eastern Kentucky with decade after decade of double-digit unemployment. As bad as climate change is, it *is* going to put a lot of people to work, and not just peons in call centers in the developing world.

Over the past 250 years, we have generally assumed that the maximum of social and economic benefit results from the sharpest, purest and most undiluted form of economic competition. Climate change is turning that assumption on its head. Not only is it simply no longer true that economic competition results in the maximum benefit, we're seeing, in the age of climate change, that it actually results in the maximum *detriment.* As the economy realigns itself and operates on fundamentally different values, cooperation rather than competition must become the norm. That'll be a big adjustment, and many economic actors won't survive in that environment. The ones who will are those who, right now, realize and accept that this is likely to be our future.

CHAPTER 8.3: BEGINNING: THE CHINESE CENTURY

Historians love to "assign" particular centuries to particular countries, empires or concepts that have extensive reach and dominance in the world. This concept doesn't always hold water—it's difficult to decide, for example, which country the 18th century is supposed to "belong" to—but one can make a case that the 16th century was the Spanish century, the 17th Dutch, that Great Britain with her sea-girding empire was ascendant through most of the 19th century, and the United States dominant through much of the 20th. It's a fairly easy call to determine which world power is next. China, meet the century that you will define, and vice-versa.

Politicians and patriots may chafe at this—the idea of the United States as a declining power is never going to be a popular one among voters—but to historians it's already largely an accomplished fact. The process began, as I alluded to earlier, in the 1970s, when the loss of manufacturing dominance transformed America's economy into largely a services, finance and information-based economy. China has taken up the mantle of the world's manufacturing leader, but it also seems poised to dominate services, finance and information technology too. Given its already outsized role in the world economy, China is much better-positioned to take advantage of the transition from fossil fuels to renewable energy and a differently-structured economy than is any other country, including the United States. Given the number of people China has to feed, house, put to work, and protect from the effects of climate change, the stakes are also higher for China than for any other country on Earth.

Historically, China is kind of an outlier: the rate at which its society changes is only outdone by the degree to which it stays the same. Innovation and tradition are the yin and yang of Chinese history. In the 20th century, the overthrow of the Qing Dynasty and its eventual replacement—over the course of a tumultuous 40-year transitional phase—by the Communist government of Mao Zedong seemed, at the time, like a fundamental break with thousands of years of China's dynastic past. Given a little perspective, though, we can see that little has actually changed. The Chinese themselves speak of their current government as "the Communist dynasty," just the latest comer in a long line of rulers that over the centuries have included the Han, Tang, Ming and Qing. And, red flags and yellow stars notwithstanding, Communism in China in 2019 is radically different than it was in 1949. You could even make an argument that

China is Communist in name only. Though they're rulers from the same dynasty, Xi Jinping has little in common with Mao Zedong.

China's ascendancy in the 21st century will probably be built largely on climate change and responses to it. The United States and western Europe have already ceded most of their political clout in world affairs to China, and China has been sucking up economic influence ever since Nixon drank toasts with Xhou Enlai at the Great Hall of the People in 1972. The Chinese also know that, on whatever basis they have built their current political and economic power, continued influence in the future will not rest on the same pillars, i.e., a manufacturing economy and military might. Figuring out how to retool their economy to survive in a climate-changed future will be the major Chinese national project of this century.

China is currently the world's second-largest economy after the U.S., comprising almost 19% of the world's economic activity (as currently measured). An unmistakable marker of China's economic ascendance would be if the rest of the world's financial markets begin treating the Chinese yuan (RMB) as the go-to reserve currency, instead of the U.S. dollar. U.S. credit in the world has been growing ever shakier in recent decades—trouble spots include the ballooning national debt and repeated political squabbles over fiscal issues like raising the national debt ceiling or funding the federal government, which used to be no-brainers but are now much more uncertain due to runaway partisanship. A significant break in world confidence in American dollars, treasury bills and debt promises seems, to me at least, highly likely, and probably sooner rather than later. When this happens, to whom will international investors turn? Inevitably toward Beijing. It'll probably be a safer investment, especially if China, as again seems likely, is doing more to address climate change than the United States.

In a way, China's turn in the world's catbird seat comes at precisely the wrong moment. After centuries of negotiating its encounter with modernity, China now stands poised to claim the mantle of world leadership that was once held by the British Empire and then relinquished to the United States during World Wars I and II. But, unlike the British and Americans, who could use their political, economic and military dominance to shape the world into pretty much anything they wanted it to be, China's leadership comes with constraints. In order to exercise that leadership role, China must lead the way on solving the climate crisis. This is why Chinese red star flags fluttering over the colonial capitals of distant lands is a pretty unlikely scenario, just in case anyone's afraid of that. The Chinese have nothing to gain by conquest. Like all of us, they will have more than enough to do figuring out how to live and prosper in a radically different climate-changed world.

China must also grapple with another problem that all of us too will eventually face: overpopulation. The one-child policy instituted in the late 1970s didn't work out so well, but as the world must learn to use less energy and generate less waste, it's also going to have to figure out how to have fewer children. China and India will get to the brink of population-related stresses faster than anyone else, but all countries will follow. When the conversation turns to overpopulation, a lot of people get nervous, and they often envision scenarios like Malthus's gloomy predictions at the end of the 18th century or Paul Ehrlich's famous 1968 book *The Population Bomb*. But keep in mind that a major population and demographic crash doesn't necessarily involve mass numbers of people starving to death or dying from some other cause. It *could* mean that, but it doesn't *have* to. Birth rates are already falling in the U.S. and most European countries. Climate change solutions must take population and birth rates into account. The Chinese will have to struggle with this issue, and eventually, most other countries will too.

The Chinese have waited centuries for true superpower status. Now, in the 21st century, climate change is handing them their leadership moment on a silver platter. They must be judicious and careful with this leadership, and they'll have to be keenly aware of the other stakeholders around the globe to keep them dancing to Beijing's tune, because they won't be able to use military force or its threat, as previous empires did, to ensure everybody stays in line. Future historians will write a lot of books about "the Chinese century."

CHAPTER 8.4: BEGINNING: A FOCUS ON INTERCONNECTEDNESS

Much of history is about economics, military power, leadership, and broad-stroke trends that we can measure, if not in names and dates, in charts and graphs like the demographic data I've sometimes referred to. But history is also about ideas, values and spirituality. Social, intellectual and religious history will be irrevocably altered by climate change as much as economic, political and military history. As with previous subjects, if we project historical thinking forward, we may be able to divine some trends in how the future unfolds.

The era of climate change is likely, in my view, to engender a significant trend in intellectual and spiritual thought toward interconnectedness, not just between people and the environment, but between people themselves. For all the conflict and upheaval that climate change may bring, I do believe it will bring people closer together. This is going to be one of the good things that climate change does for us.

The history of thought and spirituality, like many other things, resembles a series of pendulum swings. In Western Europe during the early and high Middle Ages, the spiritual landscape was dominated by the Catholic Church, and Christianity was tightly administered from the top down by bishops controlled from Rome. One of the major effects of the Black Death pandemic of the 14th century—which wiped out a third to perhaps even a half of Europe's population in just four years—was a profound and deep crisis of faith. Why did God punish the world with such a pestilence? What did the people who suffered and died do to deserve it? The Roman bishops had no easy answers. The pendulum swung in the 15th and particularly 16th centuries away from religion as a centralized concern, and into a more democratic, less monolithic and do-it-yourself form of worship, which eventually came to be called the Protestant Reformation. Ideas about God and humanity changed profoundly as a result.

Let's take another example on a smaller scale. In the United States in the 1960s, traditional belief systems were challenged on many fronts by the Civil Rights Movement, feminism, reaction to the Vietnam War and the development of youth culture. Many people came to question whether women belonged in the kitchen, whether Native Americans belonged on reservations, and whether LGBT people belonged in the closet. Alternative spiritual movements also grew during this period, with a lot of public interest in everything from transcendental meditation practiced by the Maharishi Yogi—who counted John Lennon among his disciples—to dark and disastrous sects like Jim Jones's People's Temple and Charles Manson's Family. Beginning in the late 1970s, the pendulum swung again. Traditional churches, particularly evangelical ones, were booming. Socially conservative figures like Phyllis Schlafly and Anita Bryant, who opposed feminism and LGBT equality, were prominent. Alternative spiritual movements started to look a lot more like kooky cults. Pendulums are always swinging one way or another.

Climate change is rooted principally in economic ideas: use and exploitation of resources, unlimited "growth" (there's that word again), and unfettered competition. There is, even now, increasing awareness that climate change is an unintended consequence of these intellectual ideas and values. It seems almost inevitable that the pendulum will, as climate change continues to pinch, swing against the values and ideas that created it. Economic competition as a force for good may become something of a quaint notion. Unlimited exploitation of resources may, and I think probably will, be viewed as immoral. We can't dig our way out of climate change without questioning or abandoning the ideas that gave rise to it.

Interconnectedness and a collective sense of mutual benefit is the opposite of the idea of unfettered self-interest and competition. Therefore, spiritually speaking, it seems that interconnectedness and collective consciousness is the antidote to climate change and the thinking that got us there. The fact that, as a practical matter, human beings must cooperate both politically and economically to solve climate change problems will make it even more likely that interconnectedness will develop as a significant societal value.

If you *really* want to throw your mind into some uncharted territory, consider how climate change might affect religious history. Pope Francis I already committed the Catholic Church, through his 2015 encyclical *Laudato si'*, to addressing climate change as a theological and religious imperative. Recasting environmental degradation and the exploitation of fossil fuels not merely as social ills, but as actual sins, is a bold frontier in theology. Whether the Catholic Church ultimately follows Francis's lead and goes all-in on battling climate change is almost irrelevant; *some* religious organization or another, be it Christian, Jewish, Muslim or something else, certainly will. You can imagine both positive and negative implications of this. A congregation of mild-mannered Presbyterians volunteering to install solar panels sounds pretty good. A cadre of holy warriors going around blowing up oil refineries to cleanse the world of the sin of fossil fuels, not so much. But, like any and every other major problem in human history, religious organizations will assimilate climate change into their belief systems, and faith-based groups will mobilize to address it.

Although climate change, as I've said, follows no ideology and doesn't give a damn what you think of it, it definitely has spiritual effects. It forces us to recognize that all of us on Earth are in this together, and that everything we do affects other people. Living in a world with higher seas, more extreme weather and more resistant diseases certainly sucks, but on the flip side, living in a world where circumstances force us to come together and see the value in one another doesn't sound so bad to me. Recognizing the benefits of climate change doesn't mean we minimize its dangers or detriments.

When history takes away something with one hand, often it gives up something unexpected with the other.

CHAPTER 8.5: BEGINNING: THE NEXT PHASE IN HUMAN HISTORY

It's one of the major tenets of this book that climate change represents a transition of one era of human history to another. From my study of history, nothing—absolutely *nothing*—is clearer to me about climate change than this. Climate change is a pivot point. And it's not a small thing, something that will only become visible if you look close up, like, "Oh, yeah, in that period of history they *also* had to deal with climate change." The epoch of climate change will be clearly demarcated in our history no matter how far you zoom out—similar to the Middle Ages, or what historians call the "Early Modern" period, or the ancient world as exemplified by Egypt, Greece, Rome and China.

Climate change will be a pivot because it's the flip side of the previous pivot in human history, industrialization. No one disputes that the advent of industrial technology at the end of the 18th and beginning of the 19th century transformed human society and culture. Before 1750, most people in the world were engaged in the day-to-day business of growing enough food to feed themselves. Cities were small, and the great accomplishments of humankind were either monuments and cathedrals, like Hagia Sofia in Istanbul or Notre Dame in Paris, or intellectual developments. Today, only a tiny sliver of humanity earns its living by farming, and one can find human footprints on the surface of the Moon. Industry made that difference, and so, to a huge extent, did fossil fuels.

But now we've received the bill for all of those awesome accomplishments. We can't undo what we've done, and, at least the positive changes that have occurred in the age of industrialization we should rightly be proud of. We know that our global way of life must change, and it will. The world is about to remake itself, and a new chapter in history is about to be written.

In a sense, you and I, who live today in 2019, have an extremely privileged place in history. Only a handful of human beings were born in one great era and died in another. Not only do we "live in interesting times," as the (misattributed) proverb holds, but we also live at the time of maximum decision: what choices are made—or *not* made—about climate change in the next few years and decades will lock in perhaps centuries of future history. All those generations who live after us, and there will be many of them, will have the benefit of hindsight. They'll know how our choices will have turned out, but they will find it hard to appreciate what the issues look like from our vantage point, without that hindsight.

It's impossible to talk about this change in the story of mankind without discussing it in very broad, and perhaps vague, terms. In this book I've tried to set out what I think are some reasonable suppositions about how climate change will shape our future, and I think there are good historical reasons for supposing that these outcomes are at least possible. It seems beyond question that climate change is now, and will continue to become, the singular issue of our time and for a long time to come. How can it be otherwise?

Whether we like it or not, we live in the era of climate change and it will define all of us in ways we never expected. One wonders how many people, in the grips of great historical crises like the Black Death or World War II, sighed in exhaustion and lamented, "Why was it my misfortune to live in this time?" Many, many people will say something like that about climate change over the next few centuries. But we *do* live in this time, and the rest of our lives will be consumed with, and dominated by, climate-related concerns. There's no two ways about that, no sugar-coating it. We must get down to the business at hand and find the opportunities amidst the serious challenges we face.

CHAPTER 9: IS THERE HOPE?

So now, the big question: is there hope? Is a climate-changed world survivable, or desirable? Do we have anything to look forward to?

Yes.

Emphatically, *yes*. There *is* hope. We can, and will, survive. Remember: this is not the end of history, but rather the beginning of a new phase of it.

There clearly are people out there who believe that climate change *is* the end of history, meaning that it will cause the imminent extinction of the human race. To say that I disagree with those people is something of an understatement. With this book now nearing its end, that this is my position should be abundantly clear to everyone.

Personally, I find the extinction argument not only factually and historically unsupportable, but morally objectionable. Regarding the question of whether human civilization is ready to give up fossil fuels and its various behaviors that have caused and exacerbated climate change, an argument that goes, "I don't think we will change, therefore I think we'll die," is simply another way of saying, "I do not *want* to change, therefore I would *rather* die." The extinction argument is an excuse for sitting back and doing nothing—the easy way out. We needn't bother figuring out how to change our lifestyle, because, quite conveniently, we'll all die soon and we won't have to worry about it. Believing in human extinction is also a sort of ethical absolution: if there will be no succeeding generations, no one will be around to blame us for doing nothing about climate change. Isn't *that* convenient?

As I've said before, this conclusion has no precedent in human history. Even if it was a certainty that global warming means the end of the human race, no society has ever voluntarily decided to submit to its own termination because it's too enamored with the status quo to think of changing. Even if individual members of a society come to that conclusion, there will *always* be a majority who favors doing whatever it takes to try to survive. If that was not a basic truth of human nature, there would have, for example, been no survivors of the Holocaust, because this faulty psychology predicts that all the Jews of Europe would have recognized that Hitler was far too powerful to resist, and they would have marched resignedly into the gas chambers with a shrug of their shoulders. Obviously this did not happen.

I have found that the extinction argument tends most often to come from three different quarters. The first are pure deniers, who don't really believe that climate change is a thing but are tired of arguing about it, so they say "Well, it's too late to change and we're screwed anyway, so why bother?" (Certain elements of the Trump administration have, on occasion, expressed this opinion). Defeatism is a form of denialism. It's also pretty disingenuous; if they don't believe in climate change in the first place, how can they believe it will cause human extinction?

The second group whom I've seen profess the extinction argument are what we might call casual misanthropes. In this camp, human causation of the disaster of climate change is usually emphasized, with extinction positioned as a just and ironic punishment. "The human race sucks, so we deserve to die from climate change." I'm personally acquainted with a number of people who profess casual misanthropy as a philosophical worldview. They tend to find humor in news stories of people who inadvertently commit suicide in bizarre or convoluted ways involving their own stupidity, such as the famous "Darwin Awards" popular on the Internet. (Everyone knows someone on Facebook like this). Climate change, seen through this light, is the "Darwin Awards" ending for the human race. I suppose I can see the black humor in it, but I'm uncomfortable with casting it in this light.

Finally, there are people who *are* seriously engaged with the issue of climate change, and who really *do* believe that we're totally screwed. It's understandable that some might reach this conclusion, particularly if you look at the ominous wave of species extinction and compare it with previous extinctions in Earth's deep history. But there are two points to be made about these comparisons. First, none of the five previous extinction events were *total* extinctions. Something always survived. (And it was not the simplest forms of life that survived; the heaviest losses in the Permian-Triassic event were in marine invertebrates). And secondly, none of these events occurred since humans gained the ability to think, reason and navigate their environment with intelligence and rational thought. In other words, that we would *not* survive a mass extinction event, in some form, is by no means a foregone conclusion. In fact, our chances of surviving a mass extinction event are probably significantly higher than most other species, because we can think rationally about how to survive and build tools to help us do so, where most other species will have to rely on instinct and biological adaptation.

But even setting aside the slate-wiping doomsday arguments that are sometimes asserted, whether sincerely or rhetorically, I believe this book has shown that there's more than enough historical precedent to inform the conclusion that there *is* hope. Because the effects of climate change are cumulative, every degree of additional warming that we can prevent will stave off another cascade of increasingly unpleasant consequences. Would you rather spend $50 trillion on a seawall around New York City to resist two feet of sea level rise, or $200 trillion on a wall to hold back four feet? These kinds of calculations, by themselves, make the case for immediate action to reduce carbon emissions. But even this is something of a depressing argument. We don't necessarily need to reach it to motivate action, because there's a much better reason for embracing change and working toward solutions.

Here's a novel idea: why don't we work enthusiastically to build a *better* world that will bring us benefits, instead of toiling resignedly, like a prisoner on a chain gang, simply to avoid suffering an even worse punishment? Isn't that a much more attractive prospect?

We all hate sitting in traffic. Think of the vast hours, days, years of our lives that could have been spent doing something other than sitting in a steel can on an asphalt road, staring at bumpers and wishing you were somewhere else. The end of the fossil fuel era will mean the end of this astonishing drain on our happiness and productivity. Who would *not* welcome this? Even a marginal improvement—say, spending our commutes in self-driving cars powered by renewable energy, where we can get some work done or relax while the cars drive us—will yield significant tangible benefits.

I've mentioned several times that a climate-changed future, bringing with it the immutable demands of using less energy and creating less waste, will probably move slower and be less hectic and manic. Much has been said in the past few decades, especially since the advent of social media, of how our attention spans have shortened. A slower-moving, less hectic future means that our attention spans will grow longer, which means we'll become deeper thinkers, more contemplative and less nakedly reactive. That's certainly a step forward for humanity, isn't it?

In our modern first world economies, we eat an awful lot of processed foods, many of which are terribly bad for us—obesity, diabetes, heart disease and various cancers are the inevitable result of diets laden with sugary soft drinks, fat and chemicals. Processed foods, especially fast foods and junk foods, are so heavily dependent upon fossil fuels that they basically can't exist without them, and without the long carbon-intensive supply chains that go into creating and delivering them. Take away fossil fuels and we'll have no choice but to eat a lot more locally-sourced food and a lot less processed junk. Climate change brings plenty of dangers to one's health, and food insecurity in the developing world is undoubtedly going to be a problem, but the fact that we can only solve those problems by eating better and eating smarter will bring benefits as well.

I've also mentioned that climate change is going to force people to cooperate more and compete less.

Whether it's Israelis and Palestinians in Gaza, North or South Koreans in northwest Asia, or Republicans and Democrats in Washington, D.C., cooperation and the laying aside of differences is a mandatory condition of dealing with climate change. Even if climate change triggers large-scale conflicts across the globe—I hope it doesn't, but it's possible—the settlement of those conflicts will have to involve some sort of reconciliation, because that's the way conflict resolution has worked throughout history. Even in the darkest hours of history people have justified sacrifice for the hope of a more peaceful and cooperative future. One of the most popular songs in Britain during World War II was "The White Cliffs of Dover," whose lyrics are all about that sort of longing.

When you deal with climate change, as I've done in this phase of my life, you learn quickly that the two dirtiest words in the climate change space are "climate optimist." Expressing any sort of optimism about a climate-changed future seems almost taboo. There's an unspoken assumption that climate change discourse must be uniformly apocalyptic, because nothing less than "WE ARE ALL GOING TO DIE VERY SOON" rendered in 12-foot-tall neon-lit letters is sufficient to motivate public and governmental action on the scale needed to meet the challenge. That's nonsense of course, but you'd be surprised at how many people engaged on the issue of climate change are instinctively reluctant to consider its benefits as well as its detriments. The other fear in expressing "climate optimism" is that, by pointing out what we'll gain, it might seem to be minimizing or dismissing the dangers, losses and tragedies that will also inevitably result. But expressing optimism or identifying opportunities isn't the same as saying that climate change is a good thing and we should welcome it.

I wish climate change had never happened. I don't feel hatred toward it—to quote Starbuck from Melville's *Moby-Dick*, "To be enraged with a dumb thing, Captain Ahab, seems blasphemous"—but if I'd had a choice I would rather spend the second half of my life writing books and teaching history than dealing with a global crisis whose implications are admittedly depressing. Often I think back to the first half of my life, when I'd never heard of climate change or didn't appreciate those implications the way I do now. Nevertheless, this is the world we live in, and this is the history we're living through. Let's make it the best we can.

CHAPTER 10: A NEW WORLD

History is, in one view, a story of renewals. New worlds arise and are built from the ashes of the old. As old worlds pass away there's plenty to mourn, and there are usually dead to bury and survivors scarred by what they've endured. But something new is always built in the place of what's been lost. This will be no less true of climate change than of any other event in human history.

Here's a story from history that shows you how this works. On the first night of September, 1666, a small fire began in the hearth of one Thomas Farriner, a London baker who provided bread for the Royal Navy among others. London was, at the time, in the grip of a ten-month drought that had desiccated everything in sight. Only a year before, in 1665, the city suffered from the worst outbreak of bubonic plague in its history since the Black Death. Farriner's little fire quickly spread and ultimately created a firestorm, like those that would be seen in Dresden and Tokyo at the end of World War II. The devastation of the Great Fire of London was hard to fathom: the entire heart of the old city had melted into ashes. But as the decades and centuries after 1666 passed, London was rebuilt into an early modern metropolis, the seat of an empire that spanned the globe and a center of culture, learning, finance and trade. The fire burned off London's medieval shackles and cleared the way for its rise as one of the world's great cities.

Something similar, I think, is going to happen to the world in the wake of climate change. The disasters that await us far dwarf the five days of fire that cauterized London in 1666. We will be forced to endure decade after decade of hurricanes and storm surges; we'll moan and swelter in excruciating heat waves that will never give us a break; our coasts will be eaten away by rising seas; many people will die from food insecurity, emergent diseases or war. But, taking the long view of history, the world of the far future—chastened and tested by these disasters—may be considerably more impressive than the one we live in now. The problems that climate change will teach us to solve, and the values we learn from pulling together in the worst crisis of our collective history, will make us a better people. I firmly believe that.

As a historian, I'm more comfortable dealing with the past than the future. But that doesn't mean I don't imagine what the future might be like, or that I don't spend a lot of time thinking about it.

Let's imagine New York City in the year 2080. And let's do it methodically, with purpose, to put it in historical context. This is not a prediction, but just an imagination.

First, think of who might be around to actually see New York in 2080. You may well be, especially if you were born in this century or within the last two decades of the 20th century. I may also still be alive then; I'll be over 100, but that's certainly possible. If you have a young relative, a child born recently, chances are very high that he or she will be around at that time. In fact, statistically speaking, I can virtually guarantee you that, unless you're an elderly hermit living in seclusion in the woods, you will encounter a human being today who will not only be alive in 2080, but well into the 22nd century.

Now let's take stock of what's likely to still be around in New York in 2080. The oldest building in New York City that still exists today is the Wyckoff Farmhouse in Brooklyn, which was built in 1652. Because this building has already proven it's capable of extraordinary longevity, it's a good bet that another 60 years won't make much of a difference, so the Wyckoff Farmhouse will probably be there in 2080. The crypt of Alexander Hamilton, which has been at Trinity Churchyard in lower

Manhattan since his body absorbed Aaron Burr's fatal bullet in 1804, is also likely to survive because there's a reason to preserve it. As among the skyscrapers, modernity's equivalent of the great European cathedrals, chances are good that we'll preserve at least one if not both of the Chrysler Building and the Empire State Building, which date from 1930 and 1931 respectively. The Brooklyn Bridge, built in 1883, is highly useful as well as culturally significant, so it's a good candidate for survival. Central Park is also unlikely to go away, especially since it was designed, in 1857, as the "lungs" of the city, and its environmental attributes will become even more important in the era of climate change.

So already we've painted a picture of New York in 2080 as being somewhat recognizable, with landmarks that will mark its identity in that time as it does in ours.

Now what will be different?

Well, we know for a fact that sea level in 2080 will be higher. The Hudson and East Rivers aren't quite as calm as Venice's lagoon, so allowing Manhattan to flood and transforming Broadway and Fifth Avenues into waterways plied by gondolas doesn't really seem feasible—so that means somebody, between now and 2080, is going to have to build a very large seawall.

It's also a fair bet that much of New York City's energy will be developed on-site. That means solar panels—lots of them—and possibly wind turbines on the higher buildings and terraces. Because sequestering CO_2 will be a priority, and trees are still the best way to do that, there may be significantly more trees visible around the city than there are now. With a decrease in car traffic, the auto-intensive spaces built for the 20th century like freeways, parking lots and car dealerships can be given over to forest and green spaces. The chirp of birds and the rustle of leaves may be as ubiquitous a sound in downtown Manhattan as car horns are today.

In a climate-changed future, not only will much (if not all) of New York's energy have to be generated on-site, but it will have to use less of it. Imagine the city is darker than it is today. Times Square is much more subdued, with its billboards and advertisements painted rather than electronically illuminated. Soft lighting, whether from LEDs or even candles, predominates in interior spaces, giving everything a sort of burnished, soft-focus look.

In an era with many fewer processed and mass-produced foods, there's a lot growing around New York. Skyscraper terraces and urban plazas are green. Fire escapes, at least in the warm months, are festooned with vegetables. You might see livestock in pens here and there: cows, pigs or goats, locally-sourced, destined to wind up on the plates of Midtown's many restaurants and in the kitchens of local residents.

Horses have made a return. Buggies and delivery carts, made from light biodegradable materials or recycled plastics, clatter slowly through the streets pulled by horses. Manure, which is needed to fertilize all those skyscraper terraces and community gardens, is too valuable to let it accumulate on the streets. The horses may wear diapers of some kind which can be quickly cleaned out and recycled at the end of a day's work. Horse traffic means livery stables, which may be as common in Manhattan in 2080 as gas stations were a century before.

Undoubtedly there *will* be at least one gas station left in Manhattan in 2080, but you won't be able to fill up your car there. It's a museum, its pumps long-since disconnected; tour guides dressed in service station uniforms give mini-lectures about how gasoline used to be delivered, every morning, to those tanks there, and how this station—one of the few that wasn't torn down—was given to the City of New York as a museum piece by the trustees of the ExxonMobil bankruptcy.

Amidst such details that may prove amusing to us today, millions of people will still live and work in a climate-changed New York in 2080, and the fabric of their lives will continue to spin the great tapestry of the city's history. Someone that you know today will be among them. They will speak English, Spanish, Chinese, Vietnamese, Tagalog, Navajo, Thai, Russian, Arabic and many other tongues. Some of them will work in industries we've never heard of and have job titles that make no sense to us. They'll have love affairs, they'll worry about their bills, and the older ones—they won't be called Millennials anymore—will curse about how the city is going to hell in a handbasket. Budding writers will still move to New York hoping to pen the next great American novel. The waters will lap at the seawall and the summer heat waves will shut the city down for days at a time while fans drone and people sleep on their fire escapes, but history will move on, just as it does now.

This is one possible vision of the future of a very small corner of planet Earth, which is now going collectively into the trial of climate change, and will undoubtedly be greatly altered by it. Imagine the whole world altered on a similar scale. The warmest tide will bring much change. We must be ready for it.

CHAPTER 11: CONCLUSION

I hope I've demonstrated in this small book that, while climate change is a monumental challenge, we do *not*, as some will insist, stand at "the end of history." We *do*, however, stand at the end of this book, and as such it's worth it to recap the few main points.

Climate change—global warming—is here now, and will be for the foreseeable future, the single biggest engine of historical change. Almost nothing in our world will be unaffected by it, and all of us will be significantly engaged with it for the rest of our lives, whether we want to be or not.

The societal responses to climate change will be transformative. It's not just a transition from the era of dirty fossil fuels to a more sustainable basis of renewable energy, though that transition, which is already well underway, is certainly part of it. Our global economy and lifestyles, especially in the developed West, are so based upon the possibilities of cheap fuel and unlimited resources that we must develop new ways to live as cheap fuel becomes infeasible and we butt up against the limits of resources we've previously taken for granted. We don't have a choice in this matter. Our future world *will* use less energy and generate less waste, one way or another.

Although in the abstract our global society has a choice as to whether or not to kick the fossil fuel habit and embrace more sustainable ways of living, in historical terms there is simply no precedent for the entire human race electing to remain passive in the face of such deep challenges. Thus, for all intents and purposes, we really *don't* have a choice. We must adapt to and do the best we can to beat climate change. Even if a minority of humans for whatever reason choose the path of cowardice by electing to do nothing, many, many others will not accept that decision. Nor should they. Historical precedents, most recently the decision by a small group of political leaders not to annihilate the human race in a nuclear war between superpowers, favors the conclusion that we will ultimately elect to do the right thing.

The pace of change is increasing rapidly due to climate change. In periods of chaotic transition between major eras of history, events often seem to occur "faster" than they do at other times, and broad, systemic change is sometimes extremely rapid—as it was, for example, during the mere four years of the First World War. For this reason, the phase-out of fossil fuels and the transition to more sustainable means of living may occur faster than many people expect.

Climate change is also driving a generational shift in control and ownership of the world's political and economic resources from the Baby Boomers to the Millennials and post-Millennials. This shift also will likely occur more quickly than previous generational shifts, precisely because the younger generations understand that time is the issue and they have none of it to waste.

As efforts to meet the climate crisis generate greater and greater urgency, humanity may find so much of its collective attention focused on climate change that other factors—like the large-scale clash of ideologies—may become less important. While climate-related issues certainly will be filtered through ideological lenses, the necessity of cooperation to deal with climate change is likely to transcend the divisiveness of ideological competition.

Try as we might, no one can predict the future with total accuracy and clarity. That doesn't mean, however, that we can't make educated guesses as to what may occur based on careful observation of patterns in the past. This is why a historian is particularly well-suited to make sense of our future as it will be affected by climate change. There are many things about man-made global warming that are unprecedented. That's certainly true. But how we react to these unprecedented threats *is*, I think, discernible through the study of history. That's the insight I've attempted to communicate here.

There's no shortage of negative effects of climate change that can rightly be called disastrous. It's going to cause a lot of upheaval, a lot of chaos, and a lot of heartbreak. Sea-level rise, competition for resources, emergent diseases, the potential for large-scale conflict—all of these are potentially on the table. But to treat global warming as a *"Game over!"* moment for the human species ignores all historical reality. There *is* hope. We all must work hard, to change ourselves as much as to change the world around us. We don't have a choice but to live in these times. History shows us that challenging times often brings out the best, as well as the worst, in individual people. Those times have come again. Let's go forward and write the next chapter of human history with courage, reason, compassion and determination.

NOTES AND BIBLIOGRAPHIC INFORMATION

Chapter 1: The End of History?

"The End of History": Fukuyama, a political scientist, first posed the question of "the end of history" in an essay with that title ("The End of History?", note the question mark) published in Vol. 16 of *The National Interest*, 1989. He later expanded the essay into a book, *The End of History and the Last Man* (New York: Free Press, 1992). The retort, "We haven't run out of history quite yet," is a line from the 1991 Paramount Pictures film *Star Trek VI: The Undiscovered Country*, written by Nicholas Meyer and Denny Martin Flynn, directed by Meyer, with the line delivered—in typical ham fashion—by William Shatner as James T. Kirk. These works are actually linked because both were reactions to the end of the Cold War and particularly the fall of the Berlin Wall in 1989.

"I've never heard anyone talk about climate change like that before": Communicating about climate change is a field that has only recently begun to get the attention it deserves. I'm often asked about it, sometimes in terms that themselves betray the problems and biases inherent in it: "How should scientists communicate climate change in a way that gets people to take action?" (This was a question posed to me by an audience member at a May 2019 presentation I gave to an association of accountants). The usual default is that climate change is something that belongs to *scientists*, whose job it is to interest the rest of us in what they've discovered. This assumption in itself shows how we instinctively minimize the problem. If an asteroid were coming to destroy Earth in 30 days, would we assume that it's the job of astronomers to tell us all what we should do about it? Certainly they'd have an input, but the assumption that climate change is the bailiwick of scientists, and they're expected to take the laboring oar in climate change communication, is a faulty one.

"Fear itself": The broader context of the quote from FDR's first inaugural address is as follows: "This is preeminently the time to speak the truth, the whole truth, frankly and boldly. Nor need we shrink from honestly facing conditions in our country today. This great nation will endure as it has endured, will revive and will prosper. So, first of all, let me assert my firm belief that the only thing we have to fear is fear itself—nameless, unreasoning, unjustified terror which paralyzes needed efforts to convert retreat into advance. In every dark hour of our national life a leadership of frankness and vigor has met with that understanding and support of the people themselves which is essential to victory. I am convinced that you will again give that support to leadership in these critical days...Plenty is at our doorstep, but a generous use of it languishes in the very sight of the supply. Primarily this is because rulers of the exchange of mankind's goods have failed through their own stubbornness and their own incompetence, have admitted their failure, and have abdicated. Practices of the unscrupulous money changers stand indicted in the court of public opinion, rejected by the hearts and minds of men. True they have tried, but their efforts have been cast in the pattern of an outworn tradition. Faced by failure of credit they have proposed only the lending of more money. Stripped of the lure of profit by which to induce our people to follow their false leadership, they have resorted to exhortations, pleading tearfully for restored confidence. They know only the rules of a generation of self-seekers. They have no vision, and when there is no vision the people perish."

"You must have faith": This quote is also from *Star Trek VI: The Undiscovered Country*, written by Nicholas Meyer and Denny Martin Flynn, delivered by the late Leonard Nimoy.

Chapter 2: What Is Climate Change?

A cold day in a warm place doesn't "disprove" global warming: Although this ridiculous argument has been a favorite of deniers for a long time, its most famous incarnation was on February 26, 2015, when Senator James Inhofe (R-Oklahoma) brought a snowball into the Senate chamber and used it as a prop to suggest that climate change is some sort of hoax. Nowhere in any scientific (or non-scientific) discussion of climate change has it ever been suggested that every place on the Earth will always, for the rest of time, be hot and that cold days and cold weather are somehow "abolished" as a result. According to this "logic," an abnormally hot day would conversely prove that global warming *does* exist. Deniers, not surprisingly, don't want to discuss this possibility.

Heavy snowfalls are actually evidence of man-made climate change: As global warming increases, there's more evaporation from the oceans which means that the atmosphere contains more moisture. Heavy rain events, like the floods in Houston in 2017, have been linked to this effect. But when the same thing happens in winter, epic blizzards can result, such as the one that blanketed Boston in 2015. *See* Joe Romm, "The Climate Science Behind New England's Historic Blizzard," ThinkProgress, January 26, 2015 (online). Indeed, although most places will see lighter *average* snowfall, heavier *individual* snowstorms are likely to occur for the foreseeable future. See Jennifer Chu, "Snowfall in a Warmer World," MIT News, August 27, 2014 (online).

"They changed the name for political reasons!": This is also a denialist trope, used, among others, by Donald Trump before he became President (in a tweet dated March 25, 2013: "They changed the name from 'global warming' to 'climate change' after the term global warming just wasn't working (it was too cold)!" First of all, note the idiocy of the conflation between weather and climate, which I already discussed; secondly, who's "They?"; and third, both terms have been used for decades, with "Climate Change" appearing in the title of Gilbert Plass's 1956 paper "The Carbon Dioxide Theory of Climatic Change," *Tellus*, Vol. 8, No. 52 (May 1956), 140-154.

The issue of how long CO_2 particles stay in the atmosphere or oceans: There are a number of things that can happen to carbon dioxide molecules once they enter the atmosphere. Most, between 65 to 80%, are ultimately absorbed by the ocean—but they take varying amounts of time to dissolve, in as little as 20 or as many as 200 years. When they do dissolve, they make the ocean more acidic; that's *ocean acidification*. Other processes, like rock formation and chemical weathering, can take hundreds or thousands of years. For a brief discussion of this issue, see Duncan Clark, "How Long do Greenhouse Gases Stay in the Air?", *The Guardian* Ultimate Climate Change FAQ, January 16, 2012 (online).

Permian-Triassic Extinction Event: The 70% figure is extinction of land vertebrates; 96% is for marine species. The Siberian Traps are one suggested cause, but that event does, according to geologic evidence, match pretty closely the timeline of the Permian-Triassic die-off. See Seth D. Burgess, Samuel Bowring and Shu-zhong Shen, "High-Precision Timeline for Earth's Most Severe Extinction," *Proceedings of the National Academy of Sciences of the United States*, Vol. 111, No. 9, March 4, 2014.

K-T Event (Cretaceous-Paleogene Extinction, or the "asteroid"): The history of the K-T Event, its discovery and how modern science has assimilated it is a fascinating story. Although it's not without controversy, several discoveries since Luis Alvarez's initial 1980 theory have confirmed that it probably did happen. For an interesting lay person's history, see Douglas Preston, "The Day the Dinosaurs Died," *The New Yorker*, March 29, 2019.

Toba Catastrophe Theory: An exhaustive discussion of this theory is beyond the scope of this book. Let's just say that the theory exists, and there's evidence on both sides. The original theory was put forth in 1998 by Stanley H. Ambrose in his article "Late Pleistocene Human Population Bottlenecks, Volcanic Winter, and Differentiation of Modern Humans" in the *Journal of Human Evolution*, Vol. 34, pp. 623-651. For a contrary view, see "Ash From the Toba Supereruption in Lake Malawi Shows No Volcanic Winter in East Africa and 75 ka" (~75,000 years ago), by Christine S. Lane, Ben T. Chorn, and Thomas C. Johnson, in *Proceedings of the National Academy of Sciences of the United States*, April 29, 2013.

Global cooling in the 1810s: This was the subject of my own Ph.D. dissertation, *Ten Years of Winter: The Cold Decade and Environmental Consciousness in the Early 19th Century* (University of Oregon, 2017). It was also the genesis of my historical podcast *Second Decade*, which began in October 2016 and continues to the present.

Chapter 3: Is It Real?

Juliana v. United States: All major filings in this case (United States District Court, District of Oregon, Eugene Division, Case No. 6:15-cv-01517-TC) are available on the website of the organization spearheading the litigation, Our Children's Trust (www.ourchildrenstrust.org). The story of the youth plaintiffs themselves has been told often, such as on a 2019 episode of *60 Minutes* (March 3, 2019) and on their ongoing podcast, *No Ordinary Lawsuit.* I've met a number of these young people personally, and they're truly amazing, courageous and dedicated people, as are their legal team headed by Eugene lawyer Julia Olson.

History of Denialism: Still the best book on the disquieting history of professional climate change denial is Naomi Oreskes and Erik M. Conway's book *Merchants of Doubt: How a Handful of Scientists Obscured the Truth on Issues from Tobacco Smoke to Global Warming* (Bloomsbury Press, 2010). Another prominent book, written from largely a first-person perspective, is climate scientist Michael E. Mann's *The Hockey Stick and the Climate Wars: Dispatches from the Front Lines* (New York: Columbia University Press, 2012). Dr. Mann, creator of the "hockey stick" graph that maps temperatures from the year 1000 to the present day—so named because of its sharp increase right at the end, representing anthropogenic global warming—has been subject to an orchestrated campaign of harassment from climate change deniers and their corporate backers. This depressing subject needs no elaboration; read the books.

This is proven beyond all doubt by documents from oil giant ExxonMobil: A choice selection of these documents, with links to the originals to download, may be found in a legal document—available online from the government of Massachusetts—in the case of *In re Civil Investigative Demand No. 2016-EPD-36* (Superior Court Civil Action No. 16-1888F), the Appendix in Opposition to Petition and Emergency Motion of Exxon Mobil Corporation to Set Aside or Modify the Civil Investigative Demand or Issue a Protective Order and in Support of the Commonwealth's Cross-Motion to Compel Exxon to Comply with Civil Investigative Demand No. 2016-EPD-36. Despite ExxonMobil's desperate and shrill attempts to invoke the First Amendment to prevent investigative bodies from compelling it to disgorge the evidence of its knowledge and obfuscation on climate change, the U.S. Supreme Court declined to intervene on its behalf, meaning that state investigations on what the oil majors knew will continue.

Implication of Shell in the same scandal: See "A Crack in the Shell: New Documents Expose a Hidden Climate History," Center for International Environmental Law, April 25, 2018 (online).

"Victory Will Be Achieved": The entire quote is, "Victory Will Be Achieved When: Average citizens 'understand' (recognize) uncertainties in climate science;

recognition of uncertainties becomes part of the 'conventional wisdom.' Media 'understands' (recognizes) uncertainties in climate science. Media coverage reflects balance on climate science and recognition of the validity of viewpoints that challenge the current 'conventional wisdom.' Industry senior leadership understands uncertainties in climate science, making them stronger ambassadors to those who shape climate policy. Those promoting the Kyoto treaty on the basis of extant science appear to be out of touch with reality. Unless 'climate change' becomes a non-issue, meaning that the Kyoto proposal is defeated and there are no further initiatives to thwart the threat of climate change, there may be no moment when we can declare victory for our efforts."

Vanuatu and climate change: For an account of the dizzying array of problems faced by Vanuatu and other island nations in the face of climate change—including evacuation, dispersal of population and cultural annihilation—see Trevelyan Wing, "Submerging Paradise: Climate Change in the Pacific Islands," Climate Institute, December 28, 2018 (online). In March 2018, Vanuatu's Prime Minister, Charlot Salwai, denounced first world nations who had refused to endorse the Paris climate accord (guess which nation he had in mind?) and proclaimed that his country was an innocent victim of climate change.

Chapter 4: How Did We Find Out About It?

General outline of the discovery of climate change: A key source for the majority of this chapter, describing the story of the scientific discovery of global warming—from Tyndall to Arrhenius to Callendar to the Keeling Curve—is a slim volume that remains, more than 20 years after its initial publication, the best book written on the early scientific history of climate change. That book is *Historical Perspectives on Climate Change* by James Rodger Fleming (New York: Oxford University Press, 1998). The addition of Eunice Foote to the story—she's usually overlooked—is documented in Raymond P. Sorensen, "Eunice Foote's Pioneering Research on CO_2 and Climate Warming," *Search and Discovery*, Article #70092 (2011), available online. Another great book that brings the history into the modern era, and is written at a lay person's level, is Spencer R. Weart's *The Discovery of Global Warming* (Cambridge: Harvard University Press, 2008). An excellent journalistic piece done on the recent (1980s) history of climate change is Nathaniel Rich's article for the *New York Times Magazine*, "Losing Earth: The Decade We Almost Stopped Climate Change" (August 1, 2018), available online.

President Lyndon Johnson was made aware of climate change in 1965: The document is called *Restoring the Quality of Our Environment: Report of the Environmental Pollution Panel, President's Science Advisory Committee* and was released in 1965. Climate change is mentioned in the body of the report, but Appendix Y4 (pp. 112-131) contains a detailed explication of the issue. It was authored in part by Roger Revelle and Charles Keeling, key figures in the history of climate science. People are often surprised to learn that policymakers were aware of global warming so early. This historical fact conflicts with the conventional wisdom we've internalized, that climate change is a fairly recent problem and did not get on the policy radar until the 1990s or 2000s. (This also conflicts with denialist narratives that climate change was a hoax ginned up by politicians, especially Al Gore, quite recently).

1957 Congressional hearings testimony: *See* National Science Foundation, Hearings Before the Subcommittee of the Committee on Appropriations, House of Representatives, 85th Congress, First Session, 1957. The testimony of Roger Revelle is found in a section titled "Effects of Fossil Fuels on Climate," beginning on page 106.

1983 U.S. Environmental Protection Agency report on climate change: That report is called *Can We Delay a Greenhouse Warming*, issued by U.S. EPA, Strategic Studies Staff Office of Policy and Resource Management, September 1983. The report was blasted by the Reagan administration as "alarmist." For background on this fascinating report and how it was compiled, see Dave Legitan, "Author of 1983 EPA Report on Global Warming Explains Why He's Still Hopeful After 36 Years of Being

Ignored," Earther (a Gizmodo.com site), March 7, 2019 (online). White was quoted in an article by B.D. Colen, a Pulitzer Prize-winning journalist who then edited *Newsday's* science section, which was widely syndicated.

T.C. Chamberlin and Roger Revelle: Thomas Chrowder Chamberlin was a geologist, but ultimately led the U.S. Geological Survey's division on glaciers beginning in the 1880s. His research on glaciers and ice ages was an important theoretical link between climate change and atmospheric CO_2 concentration. Revelle was a near-legendary oceanographer who spent much of his career at Scripps Institute of Oceanography, and he helped develop scientific understanding of the role of the oceans in the carbon cycle. Revelle was instrumental in establishing the systematic measurement of atmospheric CO_2 at Mauna Loa Observatory in Hawaii, which was done by Charles Keeling and formed the basis of the famous "Keeling Curve." For more on this history, see Fleming, *Historical Perspectives on Climate Change.*

Chapter 5: When Did It Start?

The stirrings of industrialization stretch back to the Enlightenment: For more on the links between intellectual history and economic history (industrialization), especially in Great Britain, see Joel Mokyr, *The Enlightened Economy: An Economic History of Britain, 1700-1815* (New Haven: Yale University Press, 2009). Although they are not technically related works, an interesting thematic "sequel" to this story, discussing many of the same trends as they played out in the United States, is Charles Grier Sellers's seminal *The Market Revolution: Jacksonian America, 1815-1846* (New York: Oxford University Press, 1991).

Another revolution, this one involving interior illumination: For a fascinating history of how the need for interior illumination fueled the whaling industry and its environmental effects, I recommend Eric Jay Dolin's *Leviathan: The History of Whaling in America* (New York: W.W. Norton & Company, 2007).

History of oil, generally: Although it's much lighter on the topic of climate change than it could be, the best book ever written on the history of the oil industry is still Daniel Yergin's Pulitzer Prize-winning history *The Prize: The Epic Quest for Oil, Money, and Power* (New York: Simon & Schuster, 1990). Yergin did devote significant attention to climate change in the follow-up volume, *The Quest: Energy, Security, and the Remaking of the Modern World* (New York: Penguin Press, 2011). The basic outline of the history of oil as I give it here is informed by Yergin's work.

South Africa gave up its nukes voluntarily: For an interesting discussion of this process—and the complicated factors that went into both apartheid-era South Africa's decision to build the bomb and the later decision to abandon it—see Lt. Col. Roy E. Horton's paper, "Out of (South) Africa: Pretoria's Nuclear Weapons Experience," *USAF Institute for National Security Studies* Occasional Paper #27, August 1999.

The majority of greenhouse gas emissions that are causing climate change are...under the control of a relatively small group: Astonishingly, 71% of global CO_2 emissions have come from just 100 major companies. More than half of *that* amount can be traced to 25 corporate entities, including ExxonMobil, Shell, Chevron and BP. See Dr. Paul Griffin, The Carbon Majors Database CDP Carbon Majors Report, July 2017 (online). The group of executives that stand between us and the end of the fossil fuel era could fit comfortably into a large hotel conference room.

Chapter 6: What Can We Expect?

The years 2017 and 2018, especially 2018, were major milestones in public awareness of climate change: Yale University's Program on Climate Change Communication characterizes the views of Americans on global warming as "Six Americas": alarmed, concerned, cautious, disengaged, doubtful, and dismissive. As of December 2018, the "alarmed" segment was larger than it had ever been, at 29% of the public, with "concerned" at 30%. The number of people "alarmed" by climate change grew by 8% in the nine months between March and December 2018. There are also a lot fewer deniers than there were five years ago: 12% fewer than in 2013, with less than 20% of the American public now either "doubtful" or "dismissive" of climate change. *See* Abel Gustafson, Anthony Leiserowitz and Edward Maibach, "Americans are Increasingly 'Alarmed' About Global Warming," Yale Program on Climate Communication, February 12, 2019 (online).

The sea may rise by as much as five feet in New York City by the end of the century: For this and many other sea level rise projections, I highly recommend the interactive Surging Seas Risk Zone Map online, where you can find such projections plotted on a world map along with numerous other data sets. If we do nothing about climate change, Battery Park may be five feet underwater in 2100.

Hurricane Katrina triggered what may have been the largest internal migration...since the Great Depression: The subject of internal migrations within the United States, especially of African-Americans, is complex and under-studied. For some fascinating summaries of Katrina-related migrations, *see* Laura Bliss, "10 Years Later, There's So Much We Don't Know About Where Katrina Survivors Ended Up," Citylab, August 25, 2015 (online).

Species are going extinct at an alarming rate: For a broad (but depressing) tour of the extinction event in which we now find ourselves, and its place in the context of extinction history, see Elizabeth Kolbert's Pulitzer Prize-winning book *The Sixth Extinction: An Unnatural History* (New York: Henry Holt and Co., 2015). This subject was also covered in the 2014 reboot of the *Cosmos* television series hosted by Neil De Grasse Tyson.

Disease is another depressing potential effect of climate change: For a basic primer on how climate change amplifies disease risks, see A.J. McMichael, D.H. Campbell-Lendrum, C.F. Corvalán et al. (eds.), "Climate Change and Human Health: Risks and Responses," United Nations World Health Organization, 2003 (online).

HIV/AIDS and the history of its jump into humans: "Viral archaeology" has made some fascinating discoveries and hypotheses in reconstructing the early history of the AIDS epidemic. For a wonky scientific look, see Michael Worobey, Marlea Gemmel, Dirk E. Teuwen et al., "Direct Evidence of Extensive Diversity of HIV-1 in Kinshasa by 1960," *Nature*, Vol. 455 no. 7213, October 2008, or, in lay person's terms, James Gallagher, "AIDS: Origin of Pandemic 'Was 1920s Kinshasa,'" BBC News, October 3, 2014 (online).

One thing we cannot expect is for climate change to reverse itself anytime soon: Climate change pioneer James Hansen addressed the permanence of global warming effects in his scientific paper, "Ice Melt, Sea Level Rise and Superstorms: The Threat of Irreparable Harm," in *Climate Science, Awareness and Solutions*, March 2016 (online), but particularly in a video associated with that paper, in which he frankly states that we are dealing with changes that will last beyond time-scales "that anybody cares about."

"Climate has changed before": This is, according to Skeptical Science (a web-based compendium of rebuttals to denialist arguments), the single most popular argument of deniers, popularized by one of the founders of the denialist industry, Richard Lindzen. Frankly I've never understood why it's supposed to be a winning argument. Yes, climate has changed before—with disastrous consequences—and it's taken a long, long time, thousands or millions of years, for the Earth's climate to stabilize after periods of mass CO_2 increases. Deniers rarely articulate in so many words that "climate has changed before" supposedly means that it will "change back" *in our lifetimes*, but that seems to be what they mean. When pressed on climate change, President Donald Trump has been known to deploy this argument. It simply makes no sense.

Chapter 7.1: Ending: The Post-World War II Order

World War II as an attempt by two powers...to knock the colonial powers...off the top of the food chain of world resources: This take on the nature of the war is similar to the argument that Germany and Japan were "revisionist" powers, seeking to "revise" the world order in their favor. This is a school of thought among historians, which you can see on display in R.J. Overy, *The Origins of the Second World War* (London: Longman, 1999).

General discussion of post-World War II economics and consumerist society: Much has been written on this topic. For a cornucopia of takes on this period and its economic undercurrents, both in the United States and around the world, see Stephen A. Marglin and Juliet B. Schor (eds.), *The Golden Age of Capitalism: Reinterpreting the Postwar Experience* (Oxford University Press, 1992).

Soviet false launch detection incident of 1983: On September 26, 1983, the USSR's early warning missile defense system detected what its computers interpreted as a launch of several American ICBMs headed toward Russia. The officer on duty in the Moscow bunker, Lt. Col. Stanislav Petrov, correctly decided that the launch detection was probably a computer bug. The USSR's military policy required launch of a massive nuclear counter-strike upon detection of any incoming American missiles, so it is not inaccurate to credit Petrov with literally saving human civilization. The incident was almost unknown until after the Soviet bloc collapsed. How Petrov, who died in 2017, did not win the Nobel Peace Prize for this, I'll never know.

The role of Russia in the post-post World War II order: Putin, the world's most powerful climate change denier (or ignorer), is an enigmatic figure that one could make a career out of studying. Some academics have. A recent book about the chaos Putin has made of the globe is Angela Stent's *Putin's World: Russia Against the West and With the Rest* (Twelve Books, 2019), as well as her earlier *The Limits of Partnership: U.S.-Russian Relations in the Twen-*

ty-First Century (Princeton, NJ: Princeton University Press, 2015).

Even the Pentagon...understands this: Despite being a world-class carbon emitter in its own right, the U.S. Department of Defense has, perhaps surprisingly, been pretty cogent about the strategic risks of climate change. If you're interested, see first DoD Directive 4715.21, "Climate Change Adaptation and Resilience," January 14, 2016 (online), which came out during the twilight of the Obama administration; *then* take a look at "Report on Effects of a Changing Climate to the Department of Defense," January 2019 (online). The Pentagon's concern with climate change seems to have survived—for now—well into the Trump era. I find this fascinating because it may be another situation of climate deniers being shy of risking real consequences. If Donald Trump truly believes that climate change is a Chinese hoax, he seems unwilling to risk the lives of America's soldiers to back up that conviction, especially since the military commanders have told him repeatedly that climate change *is* a legitimate security threat.

Five world wars: Historians and analysts differ on how many "world wars" there have been because defining "world" is harder than it seems. If you define wars solely in terms of magnitude—the number of people killed—you could add to my list the Taiping Rebellion in China in the mid-19th century, which at a body count of 40 million was more lethal than World War I and not quite as bad as World War II. But of course that happened only within one country. For ruminations on this kind of thing, see the latter chapters of the somewhat-dated but still instructive book by James F. Dunnigan and Austin Bay, *A Quick & Dirty Guide to War: Briefings on Present and Potential Wars* (New York: Quill and W. Morrow, 1991).

Chapter 7.2: Ending: The Era of Fossil Fuels

Documents from Exxon's files: I have already mentioned the infamous ExxonMobil documents. They actually fall into two categories: what Exxon did publicly, in the 1970s and part of the 1980s, and then what they tried—and failed—to keep secret after 1989 when the pivot to denialism began in earnest. Once upon a time, Exxon was responsible on the issue of climate change, and its in-house scientists studying what was then usually called "the greenhouse effect" or "the CO_2 problem" often partnered with government or university scientists on climate change studies. Many of those documents were public, or at least not concealed. Exxon canned much of its scientific staff when oil prices crashed in the mid-1980s. The year 1989 was the crucial turn. After that point, they went all-in on denial. The website Inside Climate News has documented Exxon's rocky history with climate change in exhaustive detail, with documents. The site also reports on ongoing court cases in which the oil giant is increasingly finding itself in the crosshairs of state governments and private lawsuits—the fate that Exxon's own executives seem to have been dreading for decades. Inside Climate News's reporting made it into a book, Neela Banerjee, John H. Cushman, Jr., David Hasemyer et al., *Exxon: The Road Not Taken* (Inside Climate News, 2015) which includes excerpts from Exxon's documents.

40 years to build a lifeboat: Exxon's initial investments into studying the phenomenon of global warming seem, according to insiders' accounts as documented in *Exxon: The Road Not Taken*, to have been aimed at proving itself as a leader in the field so as to get a "seat at the table" if and when government regulation to curb CO_2 emissions began to take shape. Serious government action was *almost* in the wind at the end of the 1980s; that's part of the story told in Nathaniel Rich's feature in *New York Times Magazine*, "Losing Earth: The Decade We Almost Stopped Climate Change" (August 1, 2018). So, while it might be fair to say that somebody at Exxon was at least theoretically *thinking* about a lifeboat, any serious effort to transition their business was abandoned by 1989.

There is an interesting metric that demonstrates that oil has already begun a terminal decline: The data cited in this paragraph and the next one is from Pew Charitable Trusts, "Fiscal 50: State Trends and Analysis," May 3, 2019 (online). While it wouldn't be fair to take this data and extrapolate from it alone an impending epitaph for fossil fuels, what I will say, not being an economist myself, is that if oil *was* entering a significant decline, this is the kind of thing we might start to see in the early phases. This is one tile in a wall of historical context that, I think, gives us reason to doubt that fossils are as permanent or dominant as we've always assumed them to be.

Britain and slavery: A seminal account of the abolitionist movement in the British Empire, with emphasis on the story of a few individuals who broke the issue out into a moral crusade, is Adam Hochschild's *Bury the Chains: Prophets and Rebels in the Fight to Free an Empire's Slaves* (Boston: Houghton Mifflin, 2005). The parallels to fossil fuels and climate change are pretty unmistakable.

I believe the collapse of the fossil fuel industry will be swift and virtually total: Few other statements I make in the book are likely to be more controversial than this one. I won't set out my reasons again for believing that we're 15 to 30 years away from a total or near-total abolition of fossil fuels, but I will say that I'm not alone. For other examples of this line of thinking, take a look at Jeremy Deaton, "The Fossil Fuel Industry's Dirty Secret: Climate Action or Not, Things Look Bad," GreenBiz.com, September 28, 2018; or Paul Gilding, "Fossil Fuels are Finished: The Rest is Detail," PaulGilding.com, July 13, 2015.

William Wilberforce, William Lloyd Garrison, Greta Thunberg: William Wilberforce (1759-1833) was a Member of Parliament for Kingston upon Hull. He was a fairly unremarkable British politician until his evangelical awakening in the 1780s which ignited a passion to abolish the slave trade, and then slavery itself, in the British Empire. Wilberforce did not live to see the completion of that struggle, but he gets much of the credit for advancing it. William Lloyd Garrison (1805-1879) was a passionate abolitionist who began the anti-slavery newspaper *The Liberator* in Boston in 1831. In its first issue he wrote, "[U]rge me not to use moderation in a cause like the present. I am in earnest— I will not equivocate—I will not excuse—I will not retreat a single inch—*and I will be heard*." Not the kind of fellow you can easily compromise with. Garrison was also deeply committed to women's suffrage, an issue with which abolitionism had significant overlap. Greta Thunberg, 16 at the time of this writing, is a Swedish girl who began, in 2018, skipping school and handing out leaflets in front of the Swedish parliament reading, "I am doing this because you adults are shitting on my future." See David Crouch, "The Swedish 15-year-old Who's Cutting Class to Fight the Climate Crisis," *The Guardian*, September 1, 2018 (online). To date, millions of school students around the world—including the ones I teach—have joined her on various climate strikes. She was recently nominated for the Nobel Peace Prize.

Car dealerships that could be turned into affordable housing: The issue of auto dealerships, in particular, is interesting. There are few starker examples of an antiquated business model than the idea of walking onto a lot, festooned with multicolored triangular flags, and getting hassled by a shady guy in a badly-cut sports coat as you kick the tires of the new (or used) cars that you might want to buy. "Take it for a test drive!" The idea of car dealerships working on this model has been widely recognized since at least the early 2000s as unworkable, but few in the industry were willing to commit to some other approach at distributing cars. This was discussed in Kees Van der Heijden's book *Scenarios: The Art of Strategic Conversation* (Chichester, UK: John Wiley & Sons, Ltd., 2005), still the Bible for scenario planning, which is a major tool in dealing with climate change. Since *Scenarios* came out, a new actor in the car-selling industry, CarMax, has appeared and basically killed off the used car lot as a cultural and economic thing. Car dealerships as a whole may disappear before too long, freeing up vast amounts of suburban real estate for more economically and socially responsible uses. I have long maintained that the extinction of car dealerships is a bellwether of climate change adaptation.

Chapter 7.3: Ending: The Age of Ideologies

MGM Grand fire of 1980 and sociologists' study of behavior: Popular conception of how people behave in disaster situations has more to do with the 1970s movies of producer Irwin Allen (*The Towering Inferno*) than it does with reality. The study I refer to specifically here is John L. Bryan, "A Review of the Examination and Analysis of the Dynamics of Human Behavior in the Fire at the MGM Grand Hotel, Clark County, Nevada, as Determined

From a Selected Questionnaire Population," *Fire Safety Journal*, Vol. 5, Issues 3-4, 1983.

Chapter 7.4: Ending: Business as Usual

IPCC Report and "Business as Usual": The 1990 report by the Intergovernmental Panel on Climate Change is where you start with any significant study of the phenomenon. Yes, it's nearly 30 years old now, but it has as much validity as a historical document as it does in synthesizing the science that existed at that time—and which has been validated over and over again since 1990. You can find it, and all the other IPCC reports, at www.ipcc.ch. "Business as Usual" is the data set for unchecked emissions at rates increasing consistently with how carbon emissions increased in the decades before 1990.

Capitalism as we've known it for the past few centuries is finished: For the BIOS report itself, see Paavo Järvensivu, Tero Toivanen, Tere Vadén et al., "Global Sustainable Development Report 2019, Invited Background Document on Economic Transformation, to Chapter: Transformation: The Economy," August 14, 2018, online (search at site at bios.fi). For an analysis of the implications aimed at lay people, see Nafeez Ahmed, "Scientists Warn the UN of Capitalism's Imminent Demise," Insurgentelligence, October 19, 2018 (online at medium.com).

"Peak Oil" and EROEI-based pessimism: For a paradigm example of this argument, see Tom Murphy, "The Energy Trap," Do the Math (weblog), October 11, 2011 (online). The nerve center of the peak oil movement online was a blog called The Oil Drum (theoildrum.com), which began in 2005, just after Hurricane Katrina, and went dark in September 2013.

Peak Oilers weren't that interested in climate change...[but] they weren't deniers: Believers in peak oil are *not* climate change deniers—quite the opposite—but they just tend not to focus on the problem, apparently believing that the end of cheap fossil fuel-based energy, for whatever reason it will end (meaning from climate change or from a failure of supply), will trigger societal collapse. For an example, see Nate Hagens, "A Net Energy Parable: Why is EROEI Important?", The Oil Drum, August 4, 2006 (online).

Chapter 7.5: Ending: "Growth"

In August 2018, British billionaire Jeremy Grantham...issued a paper: See Jeremy Grantham, "The Race of Our Lives Revisited," GMO White Paper, August 1, 2018 (online, start at www.gmo.com). Note, there are both long (full) and short versions of this paper available. The conclusions about externalities meaning that our economies are actually shrinking are in the long version (page 3-4).

"Stranded assets problem" and $24 trillion time bomb: This is what *really* keeps oil execs up at night. For a basic primer on stranded assets, what they are and what it means, see Carbon Tracker, "Unburnable Carbon 2013: Wasted Capital and Stranded Assets" (online, search at www.carbontracker.org). The $24 trillion figure is outlined in Simon Dietz, Alex Bowen, Charlie Dixon et al., " 'Climate Value at Risk' of Global Financial Assets," *Nature Climate Change* Vol. 6 (2016).

Pets.com was one of the hottest companies in America: The dollar figures in this section come from news articles in the dot-com era, specifically "Pets.com Raises $82.5 Million in IPO," Cnet, February 10, 2000 (online), and Richard Richtmyer, "Pets.com at its Tail End," CNN Money, November 7, 2000 (online).

Home ownership rates: This is a moving target because the numbers change depending on who (which homeowners) you measure, and their age groups, but it's pretty clear that numbers are down in general. See Derick Moore, "Older Buyers Near Pre-Recession Levels," Census.gov, August 13, 2018 (online).

Significantly greater numbers of people are exiting the workforce...than the number of people...who are about to enter it: As a historian I'm not as moved by numbers as some, but I found this—and the economist who showed it to me found this—deeply concerning. The numbers, again, are from Pew Trusts but based on U.S. Census data. In the year 2000, there were 13.4 million people aged 55 to 59 in the American workforce, that is, about to leave work (assuming most of them retire about 65), while at the same time there were 19.9 million people aged 15 to 19, about to enter the workforce. Thus, when George W. Bush was running for President and *Gladiator* was in cineplexes, there were 6½ million workers ready to replace the ones leaving. By 2017, there were 22 million people aged 55-59, but only 21.1 million aged 15-19, a shortfall of 900,000. Given that younger people generally work for lower wages and pay less taxes than those at the end of their careers, that means there will be considerably less money in the economy in the near future. And that's not a temporary state of affairs: the numbers of people in the next-youngest five-year brackets (age 10 to 14, meaning those born between 2003 and 2007, school-aged kids 5 to 9, born between 2008 and 2012, and toddlers under five born since 2012) are all *fewer* than the brackets in front of them, which means when *they* enter the workforce, in their diminished numbers, there'll be even fewer workers toiling away at entry-level jobs. Add to this the fact that Millennials are having many fewer children than previous generations—a situation itself exacerbated by climate change—and you see the problem. Apparently this situation has never happened before in the history of the U.S. economy.

Chapter 7.6: Ending: Ownership of the World by an Older Generation

A general word about generations: To astute readers, this subchapter will make me look like a dyed-in-the-wool booster of what's called the Strauss-Howe Generational Theory, developed by sociologists William Strauss and Neil Howe initially set out in their book *Generations: The History of America's Future, 1584 to 2069* (New York: William Morrow & Company, 1991) and its various follow-ups. While I admit I do accept some of Strauss and Howe's theories and I've adopted some of their terms, especially in naming generations, I don't accept them wholesale, nor do I entirely disagree with critiques of the theory likening it to "pseudohistory" or astrology. I think there are commonalities between members of generations, and generational identity does exist though of course it's not universal and you can't paint everybody with the same brush. Proceed through this subchapter with these caveats: talking about generational shifts, even in terms of the some of the buzzwords used by Strauss and Howe, is (for me at least) more of a historical shorthand than a full-throated endorsement of everything they claim, or everything others, not always accurately, think they see in the work of Strauss and Howe.

Nine presidents before a permanent generational shift occurred: "Permanent" is the wiggle word here, and I put it in to explain the presence of Martin Van Buren, the first President born after the Declaration of Independence (he joined the human race in 1782). Van Buren preceded Harrison. The generation that succeeded the revolutionaries—what you might call the "Early Republic generation," people born in the first few decades of the existence of the United States—stocked the White House from April 1841, when Harrison croaked of pneumonia after a month in office, until that fateful night at Ford's Theater 24 years later. That generation included Tyler (born 1790), Polk (1795), Taylor (1784), Fillmore (1800), Pierce (1804), Buchanan (1791), and Lincoln (1809). With the exception of Lincoln, this generation did not particularly distinguish itself by its leadership skills.

Likely that Millennials will permanently seize political and economic power: The ominous subtext to this notion is that, if this shift of power is not accomplished through elections and economic transactions, it may occur by violence—a revolution, in other words. I've heard futurists talk about the possibility of a revolution sparked by climate change, and, as much as I would *not* like to see power and ownership transferred in that way, as a historian I can't discount the possibility that it could happen. Look again at the words on the leaflets Greta Thunberg passed out in front of the Swedish parliament in her early days of protesting: "I am doing this because you adults are shitting on my future." There's undeniable resentment in that message. History shows us that revolution and war usually go together, so I consider this dark possibility linked to my thoughts, expressed in Subchapter 7.1, about the possibility of a third world war based on climate change.

Chapter 8.1: Beginning: The World of the Millennials

The beginning of the Millennial generation is usually defined as 1982: This bracket was established—you guessed it—by Strauss and Howe, in *Millennials Rising: The Next Great Generation* (New York: Vintage Original, 2000).

If there's one thing that Millennials hate more than climate change, it's debt: You could also substitute the word "fear" for "hate" in this sentence and still be right. See Shawn M. Carter, "One Financial Fear Scares Millennials Even More Than Death," CNBC, November 8, 2017 (via Medium.com).

Older politicians seeking Millennials' votes are already figuring out this [cancelation of student loan debt] is a sure winner: In the early stages of the 2020 Presidential campaign cycle, candidate Elizabeth Warren proposed exactly this. See Astead W. Herndon, "Elizabeth Warren's Higher Education Plan: Cancel Student Debt and Eliminate Tuition," *The New York Times*, April 22, 2019 (online).

Chapter 8.2: Beginning: A Cooperative Economy

General background of this chapter: The ideas in this chapter are pretty common among futurists examining how our economy must change in response to global warming, and you can find many exemplars of it. For a version that draws from the holistic futurism of Buckminster Fuller, the work of David Houle is prescient. See David Houle & Tim Rumage, *This Spaceship Earth* (David Houle & Associates, 2015), and David Houle & Bob Leonard, *Moving to a Finite Earth Economy—Crew Manual: The Three Economies* (Amazon Kindle, 2019).

The New Deal and the American social compact: Libraries have been written about the New Deal, its ideological underpinnings, and the endless battle among historians about how "radical" or "conservative" it was. If you want to dip a toe into these waters, you could do worse than to start with William H. Chafe, *The Achievement of American Liberalism: The New Deal and its Legacies* (New York: Columbia University Press, 2003).

Jobs in the solar industry can't be outsourced: See Terry Taminen, "Residential Solar is the Best Deal in Town," Leonardo DiCaprio Foundation, July 26, 2018. The economics of the solar industry appears, in the short term, more volatile than it is, mainly because of the issue—hot at this writing—of Trump Administration tariffs on the import of solar panels made in China which has slowed job growth in the solar sector. That doesn't really have much to do with what I'm talking about here, which is the long-term stability of renewable energy as an industry. Our solar panels don't have to come from China.

Chapter 8.3: Beginning: The Chinese Century

China's economy in general: This subject is so big and so complex that I can do little more than simply scratch the surface of it. For an interesting take on China's long-term economic strategy which is rooted in historical context, see Sit Tsui, Erebus Wong, Lau Kin Chi et al., "One Belt, One Road: China's Strategy for a New Global Financial Order," *Monthly Review*, Vol. 68, Issue 8 (January 2017). There are some interesting thoughts on the relationship between China's economic power and its Communist ideology in Steven Rosefielde & Jonathan E. Leightner, *China's Market Communism: Challenges, Dilemmas, Solutions* (New York: Routledge, 2018).

"Communist Dynasty"...China is Communist in name only: See Justin Fox, "This Chinese Dynasty Needs a Name," Bloomberg News, July 8, 2016 (online).

China is currently the world's second-largest economy: These statistics come from the International Monetary Fund, which is one of many organizations that has searchable online databases of economic performance.

If the world's markets begin treating the Chinese yuan (RMB) as the go-to reserve currency: See "BOE's Carney Sees the U.S. Dollar Eventually Losing its Reserve-Currency Status," MarketWatch, January 10, 2019 (online). Mark Carney, Governor of the Bank of England, stated that "ultimately we will have reserve currencies other than the U.S. dollar," and named the yuan as an alterative.

Malthus's gloomy predictions...or Paul Ehrlich's *The Population Bomb:* Thomas Malthus in 1798 suggested a massive crash in the world's population was imminent as the number of people being born outstripped the capacity of societies to grow enough food to feed all of them. His view turned out not to be accurate because, not long after 1798, the world's agricultural capacity suddenly grew immensely, in part because of industrialization and fertilizers. Paul R. Ehrlich, a biologist from Stanford University, wrote *The Population Bomb* (New York: Ballantine Books, 1968), which essentially made the same argument that Malthus did. Ehrlich's projections were more specific than Malthus's, envisioning massive famines in the 1970s which of course didn't happen. *The Population Bomb*, however, was more of a failure in terms of marketing and the public consciousness than it was substantively wrong about the basic dynamics of population growth. Capturing public and media attention in the disaster-obsessed late 1960s with its arresting title, *The Population Bomb* elicited understandable *schadenfreude* when Ehrlich's ideas, spun as hard-and-fast predictions, turned out not to happen.

This is actually somewhat unfortunate, as some of the cruder climate deniers out there sometimes try to argue that climate change is today's equivalent of *The Population Bomb* and will suffer the same fate. This idiotic argument ignores that *The Population Bomb* was a single book, written by one guy (and his wife, Anne Erhlich) which happened to garner some media attention, where climate change is a vast field of scientific study supported by mountains of irrefutable evidence. Unfortunately, reaction to *The Population Bomb* did much to poison public discussion, at least in the United States, of issues relating to overpopulation, which are clearly linked to climate change.

Chapter 8.4: Beginning: A Focus on Interconnectedness

General background of this chapter: The spiritual, interpersonal and intergenerational dimensions of climate change are aspects of the crisis that are starting to get a lot of attention. The aforementioned *This Spaceship Earth* by David Houle and Tim Rumage deals a lot with these themes, positing a change in human consciousness as both an impetus for and the result of a change to a circular or cooperative economy. The intergenerational aspects are dealt with in Wilford Welch's book *In Our Hands: A Handbook for Intergenerational Actions to Solve the Climate Crisis* (In Our Hands, 2017).

Effects of the Black Death pandemic of the 14th century: My favorite book on this subject is Norman F. Cantor's *In the Wake of the Plague: The Black Death and the World it Made* (New York: Free Press, 2001).

Pope Francis's 2015 encyclical *Laudato si':* The encyclical, subtitled "On Care for our Common Home," is a complicated document—to the surprise of many who actually read it, especially if their only experience of it is media coverage. It's freely available online in Latin and English. *Laudato si'* is about much more than just climate change, and in it Francis makes the case for treating the problem of global warming as being inextricably bound up in the problems of caring for the poor and preserving basic human dignity. It's also extremely dense with theology. I consider *Laudato si'* to be, along with the original 1990 IPCC Report, one of the most important documents in the history of climate change. It is worth reading in its entirety—a great deal is missed by reading only excerpts or summaries.

Chapter 8.5: Beginning: The Next Phase in Human History

The next phase in human history: Gene Roddenberry, the creator of *Star Trek*—referenced several times now—was an unabashed optimist about the long-term future of the human race. Though I have no idea whether he understood or knew about climate change before his death in 1991, I think that if Roddenberry had grappled with the issue he would still have been reluctant to alter the statement, authored by him, that appears at the end of the first *Star Trek* movie, *Star Trek: The Motion Picture* (Paramount Pictures, 1979): "The human adventure is just beginning."

Misattributed proverb, "May you live in interesting times": This quote—sometimes called a curse rather than a proverb—did not come from ancient China as is usually claimed. It was used first apparently by a British politician, Austen Chamberlain, in 1936. For the provenance and research on the origin of the saying, search for "may you live in interesting times" on Quote Investigator online (quoteinvestigator.com).

Chapter 9: Is There Hope?

There clearly are people out there who believe that climate change...will cause the extinction of the human race: For an example of a reasoned and intellectual argument that climate change is the ultimate "game over," see "Facing Extinction" by Catherine Ingram (online). While well-intentioned and touching, I feel it is an argument fatally flawed by its disconnection from historical context.

"Well, it's too late to change and we're screwed anyway, so why bother?" (as a denialist argument): This is sometimes classified as the "end stage" of climate denial. See Dana Nuccitelli, "The 5 Stages of Climate Denial are on Display Ahead of the IPCC Report," The Guardian, September 15, 2013 (online).

People who *are* engaged with the issue of climate change, and who really *do* believe that we're totally screwed: A recent review by Roy Scranton of two climate change books, Bill McKibben's *Falter* and David Wallace-Wells's book-length expansion of his *The Uninhabitable Earth* article, essentially takes this view. Scranton dismisses what little optimism exists in the final chapters of Wallace-Wells's book by noting, "He doesn't spend much time thinking about the practical steps such policies would require. He doesn't think much about how politics and governance work." See Roy Scranton, "No Happy Ending: On Bill McKibben's 'Falter' and David Wallace-Wells's 'The Uninhabitable Earth," *Los Angeles Review of Books*, June 3, 2019 (online). Presumably a version of Scranton's criticism could be leveled at me, but there's a faulty logic at work here: the assumption that "how politics and governance work" is static and unchangeable. If the argument is that the global political and economic system isn't up to the task of adapting to climate change, I would agree. But to stop there and proclaim "Game over, then!" doesn't follow logically, because how politics and governance works change over time—sometimes quickly and radically. The Imperial Russian state, at the beginning of the 20th century, was completely incapable of managing the basic functions of Russian society at that time, especially when put under the strain of World War I. "How politics and governance work[ed]" in Russia changed very fast, especially in the seven months between March and November 1917. This is not a prediction of revolution in response to climate change—though I have admitted that's certainly a possibility—but it's a historical example of how the same sort of systemic inadequacy to handle existential problems subsequently forces change in the systems in place. This is my entire argument in this book. For another take, and some support for my critique of the extinctionist narrative, see Mike Hulme, "I am a Denier. A Human Extinction Denier," Climate Home News, April 6, 2019 (online).

[W]here most other species will have to rely on instinct and biological adaptation: I do not believe that humans are the only species on Earth capable of rational thought, nor the only intelligent species. Although they don't use tools or externalize their intelligence the way that we do, it seems clear to me that dolphins and whales are every bit as capable of rational thought as humans are, and consequently their chances of surviving a mass extinction event are probably also higher than many others. The fascinating possibility of an inter-species communications breakthrough, where we can actually exchange complex ideas with whales and dolphins, may itself hold possibilities for dealing with climate change. If you could ask a whale to share his or her wisdom on surviving environmental challenges, imagine what new insights we might gain.

Chapter 10: A New World

The 1666 Great Fire of London and Thomas Farriner: For a wonderfully readable book on the Great Fire of London, how it started and progressed and how it changed London's history, see Neil Hanson, *The Dreadful Judgment: The True Story of the Great Fire of London, 1666* (London: Doubleday, 2001).

Chapter 11: Conclusion

General comment on this chapter: This chapter is intended as a summation of the basic arguments of this book. There are many books that I think are extremely helpful in understanding climate change, where we're headed and where we've been. I have cited all of them here, but if I were to pick out ten sources that I think are the most useful for understanding the issue, they would be the following:

Neela Banerjee, John H. Cushman, Jr., David Hasemyer et al., *Exxon: The Road Not Taken* (Inside Climate News, 2015)

James Rodger Fleming, *Historical Perspectives on Climate Change* (New York: Oxford University Press, 1998)

ABOUT THE AUTHOR

Sean Munger is a professional speaker, consultant, author, and teacher. He holds a Ph.D. in environmental history from the University of Oregon and a J.D. from Tulane Law School. He practiced commercial law in the Pacific Northwest for many years before he became an expert on climate change and its history. He is now especially engaged in helping business leaders understand and prepare for climate change and its effects. In addition to his climate change work, Dr. Munger teaches history in both traditional and non-traditional settings, and has taught students from middle school to senior citizens.

The Warmest Tide is his first nonfiction book. His works of fiction, in various genres, include *Jake's 88, The Valley of Forever, Zombies of Byzantium, February Romance* and the forthcoming *Eyes of War*. He is also the host and producer of the historical podcast *Second Decade*, about the decade of the 1810s.

www.seanmunger.com